My Son, The Killer

The untold story of Luka Magnotta and '1 lunatic 1 ice pick'

BRIAN WHITNEY
with Anna Yourkin

WILDBLUE
PRESS

WildBluePress.com

MY SON, THE KILLER published by:
WILDBLUE PRESS
P.O. Box 102440
Denver, Colorado 80250

WILDBLUE PRESS is registered at the U.S. Patent and Trademark Offices.

ISBN 978-1-947290-95-2 Trade Paperback

ISBN 978-1-947290-94-5 eBook

Interior Formatting/Book Cover Design by Elijah Toten
www.totencreative.com

My Son, The Killer

TABLE OF CONTENTS

A NOTE FROM ANNA YOURKIN

Before I begin to tell my family's story, I want to address the fact that I have never publicly expressed my condolences to the Lin family. I would like to take this opportunity to do so now. My entire family expresses our deepest condolences to your family for the loss of your son Jun Lin.

Anna Yourkin

AUTHORS NOTE

I interviewed Luka Magnotta for this book, both through mail and on the telephone. Any words seen in italics, whether they are at the beginning of chapters or in the body of them, is a direct quote from Luka to me.

Much of the information in this book is based on the Forensic Psychiatric Evaluation completed by Dr. Joel Watts in 2014 that was used to evaluate Luka Rocco Magnotta for trial.

All chapters titled "Anna" were written by Anna Yourkin, Luka Magnotta's mother.

Brian Whitney

INTRODUCTION

People's lies make me feel different from the rest of society. The lies separate me from them—Luka Magnotta

There was no part of me that wanted to watch *1 Lunatic 1 Icepick.*

You can find some terrible things on the Internet. If you find yourself bored and spending your time surfing around the net, you might wind up going into some dark places, like many people do. If so you might come across *3 Guys 1 Hammer,* a murder video filmed by, and starring the Dnepropetrovsk Maniacs, who are a brutal pair of Ukrainian serial killers who have since been apprehended. The video features them bashing in a man's head with a hammer and stabbing him in the eyes.

They did if for fun. The violence was less troubling than the unfettered joy the killers took in murdering a helpless man. The video is extremely unsettling on every level, but it wasn't meant to be seen by anyone but the killers. To them it was a personal keepsake, a trophy so to speak, something for these lunatics to get off on when they are sitting around the house with nothing to do, when they weren't busy killing people.

This was different. *1 Lunatic 1 Icepick* was more than an incredibly disturbing murder video that featured acts of necrophilia and cannibalism, it was a snuff film meant by its maker to be seen by millions. To Luka Magnotta, the director and one of the stars of the video, the other being his victim Jun Lin, it seemed that the killing itself was meant to be secondary to the reaction the act would receive. Although he denied it to me numerous times, on the phone and in writing, it seems to many that Luka butchered a man and abused his corpse mostly because he wanted to mess with people's heads, and to be famous, for something. Even something such as this.

Traditionally makers of such atrocities tried to keep such things underground. In the book *Killing for Culture* author David Kerekes says that *"*Snuff films depict the killing of a human being — a human sacrifice (without the aid of special effects or other trickery) perpetuated for the medium of film and circulated amongst a jaded few for the purpose of entertainment. Magnotta had no interest in performing for the jaded few; he wanted the world to see what he had done. *1 Lunatic 1 Icepick* was his opus on violence, murder, and depravity, and he made sure that it made him a star.

He even had a marketing campaign to make sure that it was seen. It is theorized that he was the person who sent the video to Bestgore.com, a shock website owned by Canadian Mark Marek, who later spent time in prison for simply putting the video on his site. Just in case that wasn't enough, Luka started sending body parts through the mail to Canadian political parties and to an elementary school in Vancouver. He had even made reference to the video by name on some of his numerous social media accounts ten days before the crime ever took place saying, "There is apparently a video circulating around the deep web and called 'One Lunatic One Ice Pick Video.' Does anyone have a copy of it?"

I am writing this book with Luka's mother. To my surprise she told me that Luka wanted to talk to me. I have spent a lifetime working with and hanging out with people who much of society finds odd, or even abhorrent. The Cannibal Cop has stayed in my spare bedroom when he was drunk. The Unabomber has criticized one of my letters to him, saying I had "the worst handwriting" he had ever seen. I pride myself on not being judgmental. I don't let things freak me out. But this felt different somehow.

I wrote Luka a letter. He responded. Luka Magnotta told me that he wanted the truth to come out. He wrote me that *"I don't give interviews. I don't trust the media at all, I have been completely defamed and slandered by them for years, the lies they've told are horrendous and very troubling. I am constantly being bombarded by news agencies all over the world to tell my story. So far, I have not. Since my mother trusts you, it will be my pleasure to work with you and help this be successful."* This was at the beginning of a twenty-five page missive, the first of many, in which he answered my questions on everything to his life growing up, his criminal history, his life as a model and an escort, and about the murder of Jun Lin.

Then I talked to Luka on the phone. He's charming. He's got a good sense of humor. We made each other laugh. I like his mother Anna. She says nice things about her son. Of course, I want to think nice things about Luka too.

When we talked he told me of how everyone had him wrong, and how he was looking forward to setting the record straight. He said *"Everything I do, I do to succeed. It's important to do things properly and right. My background has constantly been edited, I haven't spoken to anyone about any of this, none of this is my side of what happened. It's very annoying. I never wanted anything to do with the NCR (Not Criminally Responsible) defense. I have no mental illness whatsoever. I had to go with it, even though I didn't want to, but my lawyers pressured me into it. I told the doctors I had no mental illness. Even now in prison I take no medications, but the lawyers said our only chance was to go with the NCR defense. I wish I didn't do it, I wish I testified and told the story my way. Everyone else had the chance to tell their story. The judge, the prosecutors, my lawyers, I am the only one that didn't get a chance to tell my side. There is a preconceived notion that I am an attention seeker or that I love the limelight. That is something that really annoys me, all throughout my life I haven't done that. I mean I have done some auditions to be on reality shows, and then people just spin that around and make it something it isn't. Or people would talk about how many photos I would have taken of myself, that was for my job, you have to have pictures taken for your job when you are a model. Information is just fed to people, and they just go with it. They just recycle it and spin it their way and edit my history."*

His history. The video is inarguably the most important part of it.

I watched it. I had to watch it. How could I write this book and not watch it?

The name itself. 1 Lunatic 1 Icepick. Compelling. Shocking. Taunting.

I hit play.

There is a naked man tied to a bed. A piece of cloth covers his eyes; another is over his mouth. Is he drugged? He moves around a little but more like he just seems restless, not like he is trying to get away. The man is Jun Lin. He is here in this room because he answered a Craigslist ad from someone who was seeking man-on-man sex with a bondage theme. That person was Luka.

There is a man next to the bed dressed all in black, his face is I had no idea what was going on, but it was clear that whatever it was must be covered with a hood. A poster of the movie *Casablanca* is on the wall over the bed.

True Faith by New Order plays in the background.

The man dressed all in black straddles the man on the bed who struggles a little, but not that much. The man in black, Luka, has one of his hands near the man's throat.

Then Luka stabs him in the abdomen with an ice pick (or is it a screwdriver?) over and over again. It doesn't seem really violent as you watch this happen, it just seems odd at this point, like you aren't really sure what is happening, like you don't know what is to come. But of course, it is violent. Extraordinarily, viciously so. Then the torso is shown, riddled with holes.

The victim is then seen with his throat slashed, there is a close up on his face, his throat bloody and gaping. At this point it doesn't seem like things could possibly get much worse, how could they? Then Luka begins to slice various parts of his victim's body with what appears to be a large kitchen knife.

This goes on for a while until there is a jump cut and you see Jun Lin's decapitated head. Luka plays with it a bit, pulls it around by its hair. Then the video shows a knife cutting into various limbs, as the corpse is dismembered. Luka plays with the limbs a bit and even rubs his crotch with one of the dismembered hands.

This obviously gets him rather worked up. One can tell this is true because he flips the headless and limbless corpse on its stomach and has sex with it from behind. Or does he just simulate the sex? Is he not worked up at all? He seems to be wearing pants. Is this just for show? Is all of this? If so what could Luka be possibly trying to show us?

I want this to stop of course. I don't want to watch this anymore. I get nothing from this. I don't even get a real sense of shock value. I just feel sadness, both for the man and his family who were destroyed by Luka, and for Luka and his family who were destroyed by...what?

Once Luka is finished pleasuring himself, he begins to cut off pieces of flesh from Jun Lin's ass with a knife and fork, which one assume he eats. He then brings in a dog (are you fucking kidding me?) to eat a little of Jun Lin. Luka then sticks the neck of a bottle up the victim's anus repeatedly before finally ending the video by taking off his pants and masturbating with Jun Lin's severed hand. One can see his face rather clearly here.

In one letter Luka wrote me *"There is an old saying, Tell your story, otherwise, someone else will and that's what happened. Almost everything reported was complete lies and spin, exaggerations and pure sensationalism."* But Luka, what is your story? What could it possibly be?

At one-point Luka was accused of making a series of cat killing videos with names like *1 Boy 2 Kittens* and *Python Christmas*, which to many, myself included, is somehow even worse than what went on in *1 Lunatic 1 Icepick*. While I did watch the latter, I never could bring myself to watch the cat videos. Some things are just too much to bear.

Luka denied killing any cats, let alone on video, saying *I never harmed any animals! I actually adore and love them!* He has denied being the star of these videos to many other people. One thing he denied at first but then later admitted was sending an email under the name John Kilbride to British journalist Alex West who was writing a story about the cat killing videos for the *Sun* in the United Kingdom.

He wrote in the email *"I will send you a copy of the new video I'm going to be making. You see killing is different than smoking...with smoking you can actually quit. Once you kill and taste blood, it's impossible to stop. The urge is too strong not to continue. You know the fun part of all this is watching millions of people get angry and frustrated because they can't catch me. That's why I love this. I love the risk factor. It's also fun watching people gathering all the evidence, then not being able to name or catch me, you see I always win, I always hold the trump card, and I will continue to make more movies. London is wonderful because all the people are so stupid. It's easy. So, I have to disappear for a while, until people quit bothering me. But next time you hear from me it will be in a movie I am producing that will have some humans in it, not just pussies."*

Luka wanted to tell me his story, and then wanted me to tell his story to the world. He wants the truth to be known. But that video.

Why would the man I was talking to do something like that? Why would anyone?

1

The people I was with in 2012 mailed boxes.
It was not me—Luka Magnotta

In the wee hours of the morning of May 30, 2012, I awoke to a thunderous banging on the front door of my home. In a panic, at first, I thought we were being broken into, but when I peered through the blinds, I saw that the street outside was lined with police vehicles and that there were several officers from the Peterborough Lakefield Police Service standing on my porch. I found out later there was also a team of officers in my backyard with searchlights, scouring my property.

I felt scared: why would they send so many officers to my home at that hour? I had no idea what was going on, but it was clear that whatever it was must be very serious.

When I opened the door, the officers asked me my name. Then they asked if Luka Magnotta was my son. My first thought was that something had happened to him, so I asked if he was okay. One officer said, "Your son's fine; we are trying to find him." Then they asked me if he lived in the home, if I knew where he was, and when I had last seen him.

I answered their questions and asked if this was about the "cat killing" videos that Luka was accused of posting online. I told the officers I had already been in contact with a Toronto police detective regarding that matter and offered to provide them with the detective's name. They didn't seem interested but wrote down the information anyway. They asked to see the last email I'd received from Eric, which was Luka's given name at birth. I also showed them the Mother's

Day card that he had recently sent me. One of the officers pointed to a photo of Eric on my wall and asked if that was him. When I told him it was, he said, "He's not as big as I thought he was."

I questioned them as to why they were here, but the police refused to give me any further information about why they had come or why they were looking for Eric. They just told me I would know the reason soon enough.

At this point my daughter Melissa called to tell me that the police had come to her house at roughly the same time as they came to ours. She and my mother, who also lived at the house with my daughter, were hysterical. Melissa thought the police had come about the cat videos, as well, but was also told by the police that they couldn't disclose any information to her. One of the officers said to her, "Your brother is a very sick individual."

We were all very upset and confused. *What the hell was going on?*

Over the next few days, our nightmare would unfold.

I couldn't get back to sleep that night; my mind was racing. There was no way for me to get in touch with Luka. A few days earlier I had emailed him, and he'd said I'd caught him just in time, that he was closing down his email and that I wouldn't be able to reach him for a while. This wasn't unusual for him to say. He switched emails often. He also moved around a lot, and sometimes I suspected he wasn't living where he said he was. This was all normal behavior for him. He told me he was leaving for California, and he was very excited to start his new life there. He said he would contact me once he got settled. He'd been sharing his travel plans with me for a while, and although I knew I would miss him terribly, I was happy for him, he seemed so excited.

Throughout the day after the police visit, I worried constantly, hoping that Luka would contact me. I asked my mom and Melissa if they had heard from him; they hadn't either. I checked my email several times to see if he had messaged me using another account. Nothing. While I was on my computer, I happened to read an article about an investigation that was currently underway. It stated that a human foot had been mailed from Montreal to the Conservative Party office in Ottawa. Hours later a second suspicious package containing a human hand had been intercepted by Canada Post at a sorting facility nearby. Later, I saw on the news that a janitor at an apartment building in Montreal had discovered a human torso in a suitcase. It had been placed in the building's garbage pile. People were in a panic.

My mind started to spin out of control. I started thinking about the conversation I had a few months earlier with a Toronto police detective. He had viewed the cat videos and had found them very disturbing. He informed me at the time that this sort of behavior could escalate quickly to involve people. The detective and I discussed our concerns, and I provided him with important information as to where I believed Luka was then living. I was convinced Luka was in Montreal, not in Russia, as he had wanted us all to believe. A Mother's Day card he had sent was postmarked from Montreal and had contained a Quebec lottery ticket. Luka tried to cover that up by saying he had a friend from Montreal send it to me, but the card was in his handwriting. I'd offered to give the detective the card and ticket to assist them in finding him. I figured they could locate the lottery terminal and the store where the ticket was purchased and find the location the letter was mailed from. The detective declined my offer, stating my information wouldn't be much help.

With all this running through my head, I had a dreadful thought. Could it be my son, Luka, whom they were looking for in connection with this crime? Had he killed someone? It started to become impossible to escape this thought.

I was a nervous wreck. Over the following days, I desperately hoped to hear from my son, but there was still no word from him.

The months leading up to this time had been rough for me; my partner at the time, Leo Sr., had been making my life a living hell since I'd agreed to let him move back home that March. He was arrested for assaulting me in June 2010, and we lived apart until March of 2012 when I made the mistake of letting him come home. The night the police came looking for Luka was no different. Leo Sr. kept me up most of the night, tormenting me, as usual. He kept putting Luka down, telling me I was useless, complaining about things in the past and ranting about finances. It was a horrible night, and I was a mess by morning. Somehow, I got my two youngest children, Leo and Leeanna, off to school. Shortly after I got back from dropping them off, my son Conrad who was twenty-eight at the time came over, as he often did, to keep me company. I loved having him around because I felt safe from Leo Sr. when Conrad was with me. Conrad and I began chatting, and I felt compelled to tell him about my dreadful thought. He was shocked, and told me, "No, Mom, Eric wouldn't do that, it's not him! Why would you even think that?" I explained my reasons and told him I heard there was going to be a news conference on TV with more information, and I was going to watch it.

That afternoon when I turned on the TV, the news conference was already underway. It was broadcast on several channels; we watched it on CNN. The reporter was recapping footage of the crime scene in Montreal. We saw shots of police officers carrying large yellow evidence bags. Commander Ian Lafrenière of the Montreal Police was interviewed, and he stated that after scouring the crime scene in Montreal, police had discovered papers identifying the suspect, and they were going to release the person's name and photo shortly. As I watched this gruesome story unfold before my eyes, I started to become petrified. Seeing this on the news at any given time would have sickened me, but with my dreadful thought looming over me, I was in an absolute state of panic. I started repeating over and over to myself, "It's not Luka. It's not Luka. It's someone else. They'll reveal the suspect's identity soon, and this will all be over!" But in truth, I was scared to death. Conrad kept saying, "Mom, stop, calm down, it's not him."

It seemed to take forever, but when they were finally ready to name the suspect, I got up and stood in front of the television. My heart was pounding, and I started to shake. I kept repeating, "Oh please let me be wrong!" The first bit of information to come onto the screen was a silhouette of a male. They then reported that the suspect was a twenty-nine-year-old male. Luka was twenty-nine! I started nervously shifting from one foot to the other, holding my hands to my mouth, so I wouldn't cry out or scream. Then they flashed up the suspect's photo and name. My knees gave out, and I started to fall. Conrad grabbed me and held me in his arms as I sobbed uncontrollably. I cried out in horror, "No, no, no this isn't happening!" over and over again. Conrad was shaking, too, as we held each other. He tried to be strong and tried to console me, but we were both in shock and absolutely devastated. As newscasters continued to talk we heard them say that a warrant for first-degree murder had been issued.

It felt like I was trapped in a horrible nightmare. *Is this real?* I thought. *It can't be!* My head was spinning as I tried to take in what was happening. Leo Sr. sat there smirking at me through it all, saying things like "It doesn't surprise me." He almost seemed happy. All of a sudden, the phone started ringing non-stop. I felt I needed to call my parents, and I wanted my other four children with me. But the two youngest, Leo and Leeanna, were at school, and Melissa was still out of town.

When I called my parents, my father had already heard the news. He was beyond devastated and at a loss for words.

My mother was so confused and distraught that she thought Luka was the one who had been murdered. When she finally understood that it was Luka who was wanted for murder. I thought she was going to die. Her voice was shaking, and she was screaming, "Why? Are you sure? No! What are you going to do?"

I had to call Melissa; I knew she hadn't heard the news yet, or she would have called me by now. I dialed her number and mustered up enough strength to remain calm. I asked if she was okay, where she was, and when she would be home. She said she was on her way and she would be back in Peterborough in an hour or two. I prayed she wouldn't hear the news while driving. Conrad and I tended to my poor little granddaughter Emily. She could sense the turmoil in the house, and she was very upset. I didn't want my granddaughter to see me so distraught. I sat and rocked her in my arms, and as she cried on my shoulder, I sobbed silent tears. Leo Jr. and Leeanna, who were thirteen and fifteen at the time, came home from school and wanted to know what was wrong. Conrad and I were speechless. We didn't know what to tell them. Still crying and shaking, we did the only thing we could think of. We told them to come and sit down in the living room, and we turned up the television and told them to watch. It was better they found it out this way than when no family was around. Like the rest of us, they couldn't believe what they were hearing and seeing. They were in shock. They flooded us with a multitude of questions for which we didn't have the answers. Conrad and I went to the kids, and we all embraced one another in a circle. As my world was falling apart around me, Leo Sr. was still taunting me with cruel comments. Unbelievably, he was taping the news broadcasts. He played parts of them over and over again, switching back and forth from the PVR to live television. I called Melissa a few more times to check on her whereabouts. She kept asking, "Is Emily okay? Is anything wrong? Why do you keep calling me?" I remained as calm as I could and said, "Just checking to see where you are." She still hadn't heard the news, and I was worried sick she'd hear it in the car. I couldn't wait for her to get home.

The phone continued to ring off the hook all afternoon: it was mostly reporters wanting a story. A knock came at the door. It was the Peterborough Police. They had planned on breaking the news to me before the story aired, they said, but they were too late. They explained to me that this was the reason they had come to the house the other night. They had been asked to come by the Montreal Police, but they hadn't been able to give me any information at the time as the investigation had just begun. I remember the officer asking me if I was okay, and I replied, "No, and I never will be!" They kept asking us questions. I can't even remember most of what they said. Conrad was handling it all at that point. I felt physically ill and wanted to just lie down, curl up in a ball, and go to sleep. It felt like I was in a horrible nightmare, and I just wanted to wake up. The police didn't stay long, and soon after they left, Melissa arrived home. She knew instantly that something was terribly wrong. I grabbed my daughter and just hugged her. Melissa was the sibling who had always had the closest relationship with Eric, and I knew this would be hard for her to hear. She said, "Mommy, what's going on? What's wrong?"

Conrad and I pointed to the television and I said, "Sit down." As she watched in silent horror, her face went white. Conrad and I wrapped our arms around her and just held her. Just like the rest of us she was in shock and couldn't believe it. We all had so many questions, but the only information we had was what was being broadcast on the television.

Then the media frenzy hit, and we were swarmed. Reporters started pounding on our door, cameras in hand. We were polite with them at first, asking them to please go away and leave us alone. We repeated the words, "No comment" over and over and over again. But they were relentless. They camped out in the street in vans in front of our house. There were reporters with cameras and tripods set up; they were in the neighbors' yards, some were even in the trees surrounding the house. I finally decided to call the police. A police supervisor came out to the house and spoke to the media, warning them about trespassing on my property. He returned to the house and stayed and talked with us for a while, reassuring us that he would come back if we needed him to, and he gave us some advice about how to handle the media. Before he left, he expressed his sympathy for the situation our family was in and told us to call anytime we needed him. He was very empathetic and helpful. His kindness was appreciated very much at the time.

After the media were ordered off our property, they began to congregate on the sidewalks and on the street outside, waiting for any sign of movement from our house. When Melissa finally made an attempt to leave to go home, she had to run to the car with young Emily, with cameras being shoved in their faces and reporters on their heels. The reporters surrounded the car, preventing her from leaving. She was forced to run back into the house.

After we all calmed down somewhat, we came up with a strategy that would allow them to leave safely without being harassed. They were eventually able to make their escape but not without the media hot on their tails. The media followed her all the way home and converged on her place, where my mother also lived. My mother was in the yard and had to run inside and hide with the children. She kept screaming, "Go away! Leave us alone!"

My brother Eldon came by my house that evening to be with me. As he made his way through the crowd of hungry vultures that circled, waiting to pick at their next victim for information, he was bombarded with questions and asked to comment. He became livid and started yelling at them: "Back the FUCK off, stay away from me, our family, my sister, and her home!" When he finally got to the door, I was

MY SON, THE KILLER | 23

afraid to open it because I thought he was another reporter. He had to assure me that it was he and that it was okay.

I sat with him that night, talking about what was going on, and what had happened, but it's still just a blur to me, even to this day. My mind was racing in so many directions, and I started to have trouble speaking and even breathing. My head and heart were pounding. At one point I grabbed my brother's hand and said, "Something's wrong with me, I need to go to the hospital." He told me, "No, you can't go out there, they're everywhere. They'll swarm you and follow you to the hospital." He held onto me and kept repeating, "Calm down. Breathe. I'm here. You're going to be okay." As much as he tried to calm me, I could see the panic in his eyes, and I could feel his own heart pounding. The rest of that night is a blank. The last thing I remember is being in my brother's arms and hearing Conrad say, "I'm here, Mama, I won't leave you." He assured me he'd secured the house. My next recollection is being in my kitchen the following morning.

The media circus continued over the following days: letters, notes, cards, and gift baskets were dropped off and sent to our home from far and wide. Messages came sympathizing with our situation, requests for interviews and television appearances, offers to write books — anything to get us to talk. Some relentless reporters, despite being cautioned by the police not to trespass, came back onto our property, though less aggressively this time, with cameras still in hand, but not rolling, in a last-ditch effort to get an exclusive story. Our entire family remained tight-lipped and vigilant. We weren't talking. As a family, we collectively agreed not to talk publicly, and for good reason. Luka had still not been apprehended, and we knew there would be further police questioning and a trial down the road. We didn't want to impede this process in any way by something we might say. We also took into consideration that Luka might be watching the media coverage. What if seeing us talking about him publicly caused the crisis he was in to worsen?

The gravity of the situation was overwhelming for me. New articles were manifesting daily in the papers and on the television, full of details, rumors, and speculation about Luka and the crime. Through it all, we sat in hiding, trying to absorb each new bit of information. We clung to each other for support. It felt like we were all in the same sinking boat. How could we help each other when we were all in the same predicament? We decided we were going to stick together no matter what. Our family ties had been tested many times before. We had pulled through the sudden death of my younger sister, Andrea, in January 2010, and a house fire in my home in June of the same year. We'd supported each other through break-ups, divorces, custody battles, criminal charges, domestic violence, car accidents, injuries, illnesses, and deaths, but nothing could have prepared us for what we were now facing. So, with our previous battle wounds still healing, we donned our armor yet again and formulated a survival plan. We were going to have to rely heavily on each other's strengths. We sought love, faith, comfort, understanding, trust, encouragement, patience, wisdom, knowledge, and judgment from one another like never before, and together we kept our sinking lifeboat afloat.

2

ERIC

Just because people are related by blood doesn't mean they deserve to be included in your life. You know who truly has your back when you're in a difficult situation. Talk is cheap, actions speak—Luka Magnotta

Luka Magnotta was born Eric Kirk Newman on July 24, 1982. His first day in this world was spent in Toronto, Ontario, as the oldest child of Anna Yourkin and Donald Newman. His parents were young, they were still teenagers in fact, and married shortly before he was born. Anna was 16 and Donald 17. Eric would have two siblings, a brother named Conrad who was ten months younger than he was, and a sister named Melissa, who was five years younger.

The family didn't have a lot of money when Luka was young, and like lots of families in that situation, they moved around a bit. Something would work out, and then it wouldn't, and they would scramble for a while. Sometimes they had to stay with either Anna's or Donald's parents, while they saved up money and waited for things to get better. Which they always did, until the time that they would inevitably get worse again. His mother stayed home and raised the kids while his dad supported the family the best that he could with a job at a local factory.

Donald often wasn't doing all that well at the time, he was later diagnosed with schizophrenia, but back then he was just thought of as kind of troubled. Things hadn't been good between Anna and Donald for a long time at that point, and they weren't getting better. When Luka was around ten years old his parents separated, and Luka and his family moved in with his maternal grandmother and grandfather. Despite this upheaval in his young life, Luka told me that his childhood was just fine. Luka claims that reporters make his childhood out to be much worse than it was saying: *The media is constantly trying to rewrite my history, life and story to fit their sensationalist narrative. I was a very happy child, particularly before the age of 11, always very inquisitive and asking a lot of questions. I enjoyed nature and spent time on our large property. We had a very large house on 2 acres with a lot of different fruit trees and I would pick and eat a lot of peaches, pears, cherries and plums. My grandmother always made me feel like a little prince and favored me. My siblings and cousins were always jealous to be honest. We also had a large family boat that seated 10 people. We would go boating and spend the summers at the cottage and the beach. My parents always tried to give us everything. We didn't have much access to other children, so we relied on each other for fun.*

Anna was single for a while, but soon met a man named Leo. They fell in love, at least what seemed like it at the time, and Anna, Luka and the rest of the family ended up moving into an apartment in Toronto with him. This did not go well for Luka, by all accounts, except for possibly Leo's. Everyone else say that he treated Luka terribly and was abusive to him both emotionally and physically. Magnotta went to live with his grandmother Phyllis when he was 16 years old, mostly to escape the verbal and physical abuse he suffered at the hands of his new stepfather. When I asked Luka if he cared to expand on his experience with Leo Sr., he replied *I won't even dignify this idiot with a comment except to say he was, is and always will be a complete waste of oxygen and by far the most useless idiot I have ever encountered.*

Luka was close to his grandmother. He felt safe with her. She doted on him when he was a child. He knew that he was her favorite and that his siblings and even his mother were jealous of how close they were. As a child and even when he was grown Luka would call his grandmother daily and has said she was another mother figure to him, while he thought of Anna as more of a big sister when he was growing up. He said that it was his grandmother that had actually raised him when he was young, that he went everywhere with her, slept in her bed with her, and at times she even dressed him in her clothes.

Anna and Luka

Much was made of the fact in the press that Luka was homeschooled, that he did not go to school until he was around eleven. If he didn't end up being convicted of a horrific murder no one might care, but instead it has become one more thing on the list of possible reasons that he became who he became. If you are homeschooled and don't end up killing someone in a very bizarre way it is very unlikely that people would think of it as odd. But Luka did, so people do. How was his childhood? *I don't think some people should be parents, looking back, sure we always had nice houses and experiences, however some people just don't have a parental instinct. The lying media has blown everything out of proportion as usual. It is sickening and quite frankly pathetic. The fact is, no I didn't have a good childhood. Big deal, get on with it. Life is too short to waste on people who don't have your best interest at heart. Just because people are related by blood doesn't mean they deserve to come along on the ride of life with you. My mother was and is a great mother. No one has the right to judge me, their opinions do not count, nor do they matter.*

While being homeschooled must have been isolating for Luka, once he went to school and was away from his mother and grandmother and around kids his own age during the day, things did not go well for him. He wasn't the most normal of boys, and while that may have gone unnoticed while he was just hanging around at home with his mother and siblings, once he was among those who were supposed to be his peers, it became pretty apparent he didn't really have any. While before he had spent time with his family where his oddness may not have been noticed or might have even been celebrated, now he was cast to the worst sort of wolves known to man. 11 and 12-year-old boys.

Right from the start, the other children mocked him and tortured him. His memories of this time are painful. Being called a faggot, being called gay, not fitting in, not being liked. Being weird. He would try to be nice to them and try to make friends, but he didn't know how, and he didn't fit in. The main thing he remembers trying to do to make them happy was to try and give his tormenters gum.

Luka at Christmas at 11 years old.

The other kids would push him around and call him names, they would call him a fag, and when he responded by crying, they would call him a baby. He was an outcast. No one would talk to him except some kids with disabilities, who Luka later described as "wheelchair kids" who were obviously not high on the social totem pole. The class monitors did nothing to help him when he was mocked. Perhaps worst of all the other kids made fun of how he dressed and messed with his hair, which he slicked back and didn't want anyone to touch. He hated that more than anything.

Luka moved and went to a different school when high school started. One might think this was a new chance for him to shine, to make new friends, or at least be left alone, but things got even worse if that was possible. He was a very shy boy, who was picked on by the other kids and dismissed by his teachers. Try as he might to hold it together, he continued to cry often at school. He hated to talk in front of the class, as he would be laughed at, and thus humiliated. Throughout it all he showed no aggression towards other students. He did not get into trouble, he did not get into fights. Instead, he felt like a fly on the wall.

As he aged he worked at being less shy and tried to fit in with kids who were cooler, who got in a bit of trouble, and were loud and brash in a way that he never thought he could be himself. He was in regular classes, not one for kids with special needs, but he struggled with learning, and his grades were bad. He would skip school from time to time but was not doing drugs and was not involved with anything even resembling criminal activity. He wasn't that different than many kids in high school. Lost, sad, a bit unwell and ignored.

Luka at 16

It was around this point that he became fascinated with Marilyn Monroe. While still in school he read a book about her that he got from the library, did a book report on her, and would watch all of her movies incessantly. He felt they had a lot in common. He thought of himself as ugly when he was younger, but now he began to think of himself like her, alluring, gorgeous, and so very sexual. Because of her he felt more secure with who he was. They were connected, Luka and Marilyn, two of a kind. He thought of her all the time.

Since he was doing poorly in school and was miserable because he wasn't fitting in, he ended up dropping out. Later he said that part of the reason he left school was because of what sounded like the onset of mental illness. That he was not feeling well mentally. That his concentration was poor. That he felt sick and was hearing things. But he didn't say that then: he just seemed like a kid who was lost, trying to find his way.

After he dropped out of school he drifted. He tried to finish his degree at an online school but gave up, he wasn't doing well. it was hard for him to concentrate. He then wanted to go to school to sell real estate, but, of course, they didn't let him in because he lacked a high school degree. So he floundered and tried to get by. He worked a variety of low level jobs, none of which lasted long, then he eventually applied to get on government assistance because of his mental health issues. He was accepted.

So here he was. Awkward. Unemployed. Hearing voices. On disability. Then he started doing sex work.

His story of how he got into sex work isn't different than many others in such situations. His self-esteem was low, and he didn't have a lot of money, in fact he was poor. He stole food on occasion, other times he was taken to food banks by his social worker because he didn't have enough to eat.

Around this time he also got into some trouble with the law. As he describes it *A complete bastard named Tony*

Minakakis, a con artist and fraudster, dragged me into his web of deceit. When he knew the police were moving in on him he moved all of the merchandise into my house and called the police to set me up.

The apartment where Eric and Tony lived was on Thorncliffe Park Drive in Toronto. Magnotta was charged with numerous counts of fraud for using the credit card of a young woman he knew to buy around $17,000 worth of products, including a television, a DVD player, and mobile phones. He spent sixteen days in jail before trial then finally plead out to four fraud charges and got a year's probation, in part because his lawyer explained to the court how significant Luka's psychiatric issues were. The young woman was a friend of Magnotta and a couple of brothers he was palling around with. One of the brothers hooked Luka up with this girl, and he began "dating" her. Luka would go into electronic stores with this girl and buy objects on her credit card. He later admitted the girl was "a bit sick and had a mental disability" and in fact, reports say that she had the mental capacity of a child that was 8 to 12 years old.

He began doing webcam work, sitting in front of a computer, chatting to, and masturbating for, lonely men. He didn't love it, but the money was okay, and he felt like maybe he had finally found something that would work for him when it came to making money. This progressed to Luka stripping at a club called Remington's in Toronto. He was scared to go on stage at first, but money can be a strong motivator when you're poor. He got his first job by going down on the owner of the club.

He worked there, dancing on the stage, for a few months, but he wasn't happy. He wasn't making enough money, not for what he was doing anyway, not for the anxiety it caused. He also thought the other dancers were better than he was, more muscular, hotter, more desirable, just better. He also appeared in a few low budget porn movies around this time, but low budget porn movies are low budget for a reason.

They pay like shit. One of the other dancers suggested he be an escort instead. And why not? The money was much more than he could make on the stage or appearing in cheap porn movies.

So he started his career as a full-fledged escort. He had a lot of stamina. He was hungry. In the beginning, he had five to six clients per day. Of that time Luka said *I made a lot of money and had a lot of fun. Extremely generous clients allowed me to make six figures easily. One even bought me a condo. It was a great life.*

A great life. Escorting was a much better fit for Luka. The clients liked him, and so did his bosses. He was willing, looked much younger than he was, and was able to last forever. He began to make between a thousand and two thousand dollars a week, which for him pretty much meant he was rich. He got along fine with most of his clients and didn't feel that he was being abused or that things were horrible. He got out of the shitty buildings he once lived in and moved to decent places, where someone of his stature should be. In one way at least, Luka was thriving. People wanted him. They liked him. They paid to be with him.

He also attempted to be on reality TV at this time. He auditioned for a show called *Cover Guy*. In his audition tape he says, "A lot of people tell me I am really devastatingly good looking" and a show called *Plastic Makes Perfect* in which he talks of having nose jobs and hair transplants done, and how he wishes to have muscle implants done to his body soon.

Luka was generous with his new-found cash. He would often help his grandmother with money, giving her a couple hundred bucks here and there, and he helped his mother when he could, because he hated that Leo Sr. controlled all of her cash and never helped her out himself. Luka even took Anna on a trip to the Bahamas one year, which was the first time she had ever been out of Canada.

It wasn't all perfect though. Working in the sex trade never is. So many people are weird and dark and ruined, and sometimes they pay people so they can do things to them. Things that hurt. Things you can't forget. He was raped a few times but knew that if he were to try and speak to the police about it, they would be of no help. Once he was assaulted and robbed by a client. He went to the police about it, they didn't care at all.

He was mostly submissive when he was working, as that fit his vibe the best, or maybe it was just that more people who paid him were dominant, or at least pretended to be when they had the cash. He would be tied up. He would be hit. He would be called names, pissed on, and shit on. He didn't like that much. Sometimes, but much less often, he would be paid to be dominant. That made him even more uncomfortable than being hit.

At times clients would videotape what they did with Luka and would put the videos online for all to see. He didn't mind so much if they did that with regular old sex, or even when he and his client were fully immersed in kink, but he hated to be embarrassed; he despised looking the part of a fool. Sometimes videos were put online where he was bound and whipped until he bled and cried out for mercy. Other times videos were put up that showed Luka being urinated on or shit on.

While the money is good, most people don't want to do sex work forever. Not only that but they can't. Everyone gets old. Everyone gets less willing. Less able. The customers see it and want you less. Sooner or later, they don't want you at all. Luka being a prostitute at 35 years old? 40? 50? It wasn't pretty to think about, and it wasn't going to happen.

He began dating a client named Ron. They liked each other. They moved in together, and Luka stopped escorting at Ron's insistence. Ron didn't want to live with a prostitute. Luka went back to escorting part time behind Ron's back as he had no money. Ron may have let him live for free, but he wasn't going to give him money too. Not only that but Ron began to have sex with other men, not only behind Luka's back, but right in front of him. They fought; they argued; they broke up.

It was time to move on.

If you don't like the reflection don't look into the mirror, after all.

3

ANNA

*As I've gotten older I have become extremely skilled
at navigating the world—Luka Magnotta*

Luka Rocco Magnotta was born Eric Clinton Kirk Newman,
a healthy, happy five-pound, ten-ounce baby boy. As a child,
he was almost always in a good mood, and very loving,
caring, smart, and artistic. Eric was close with his younger
sister Melissa, but he and his younger brother Conrad didn't
always get along. Eric is ten and a half months older than
Conrad, and Luka would often instigate problems for his
younger brother. At times it seemed his favorite thing to
do was to blame things on Conrad and deny having any
involvement in what happened, but Luka always doted on
Melissa. As a parent I chalked up Eric's behavior toward
Conrad as sibling rivalry. My mother adored Eric and always
took his side in any dispute, and this bothered me and the
other children; my father was loving, kind and fair to all his
grandchildren.

As the boys approached school age, it was decided they
were going to be homeschooled. Later, much was made in
the press of the fact that my son didn't go to school until the
sixth grade. My husband, Luka's father Don, told everyone,
our family, friends and neighbors, who inquired about
the children being homeschooled that it was all my idea.
It wasn't. He even lied about this in court during Luka's
murder trial.

Luka at one

In reality it was my husband Don's idea. He insisted on it. Don didn't like being a part of society He had idiosyncratic beliefs and was delusional and paranoid. Life with him was like being in a cult. He was our feared leader, and we were the conditioned, compliant followers. Don was a proud Nazi/Hitler/Aryan-nation enthusiast and was your typical garden variety racist. This behavior wasn't new to him, he used to hang up swastikas in his room as a teenager. Don never really fit in anywhere, not even in his family. He was a loner all his life. He wanted nothing to do with any of our children going to school. He hated the conventional school system. He didn't want our children to be a part of "normal society" and thought that going to school would poison their minds. Don couldn't hold down a job for very long. He would quit or get fired, but when it happened it was always someone else's fault, never his.

Don was not a good father to put it mildly. He was verbally abusive to all three children, especially Eric, whom he often called a little faggot. He would slap the children. would grab them roughly and shove and push them around. He was even more abusive toward me. He would push me, shove me, punch me, slap me, and pull my hair. One time he choked me until I passed out. If he wanted sex he would just take it, forcing himself on me against my will. He controlled all of my money and what I did on a day-to-day basis. One day he even held me at gunpoint.

My life was a nightmare. He controlled my every move. He isolated me from everyone except his family, not letting me talk to those in my own. He achieved his demands through threats of harm to me and to my loved ones, intimidation, abuse, and fear. I feared for my life, my children's lives, and my family members' lives. He had me convinced if I ever tried to leave him, he would kill one or all of us and then himself. I was young, naïve, and scared to death. I honestly believed there was no way out of that relationship without casualty. I never opened my mouth to anyone about the abuse and threats. When he finally decided my family was allowed back into my life, I was already so conditioned by him and submissive that I never told my family anything about how horribly we were being treated. Even when my family members confronted me about marks or bruises on my body, I always had a story for how they got there.

It is hard for me to explain at this point how I fell for this man in the first place, but I did, and once we were together and eventually had three children, I saw no way out. For many years we lived this way. Over the years Don's behavior became increasingly hostile, not to mention violent, especially when he drank alcohol.

Things continued to unravel. Don didn't make the mortgage payments on our new home in Bethany, Ontario, for several months, and we lost the house and had to move back to Toronto and stayed with his family. Around this time Don hit rock bottom. He had lost his job for stealing from the company he worked for. He couldn't find another job, and he became even more hooked on booze than ever. He sat around the house in a drunken stupor every day. He became extremely self-absorbed in his misery, paying less attention to the rest of us.

He offered no resistance when I took the opportunity presented by his depression to enroll the three children into the public-school system. I immediately became involved with volunteering at my children's school to help the kids with their transition to a new way of life. This was my first step towards freedom. For the first time, all of us were involved with other people and out of Don's complete control.

All three children had difficulties integrating into the conventional education system, but Eric suffered the most. He was picked on, bullied, teased, and physically and emotionally abused by other students. In short, he was tormented. Conrad adjusted rather quickly to his new life while Melissa had huge separation anxiety issues at first. The anguish my children were going through impacted me greatly. I was overcome with guilt, sadness, regret, anger, and frustration.

It was an ongoing battle for Eric, he just didn't fit in with the other kids. The teaching staff, principal, vice-principal, and support staff worked with Eric and me to resolve the problems he was encountering, but the problems continued. Some of the students were cruel and persistent despite the consequences the school was putting on them. Bullying had a huge impact on Eric's life then; it was something that haunted him for a long time, although Eric did manage to make friends with a few nice students who treated him with kindness and respect.

After a lot of soul searching and work on myself, I finally had enough strength to leave their father in 1995. Eric made new friends with a lot of kids in our new apartment building, and some of them even went to his new junior high school. But once school started things changed. Eric still struggled to fit in, he was teased and called names for the way he dressed and how he wore his hair. He always wore nice jeans and t-shirts and his favorite jacket that he really liked. He used to slick back his hair which apparently was too much for his classmates to handle. To me he looked great. Eric was and still is very handsome, and I respected him doing his own thing when it came to how he dressed. He wasn't only teased at school though. As Eric approached his adolescent years, he was ridiculed by members of our own family for the way he did his hair and for his personal style. They made him feel very uncomfortable and self-conscious and constantly chipped away at his self-esteem. On the other hand, Conrad and Melissa were adjusting quite well to their new school and home and were making lots of new friends.

I met a man named Leo Belanger, things got serious pretty quickly, and I became pregnant with his child. It pains me to admit it, but I had yet to learn to love myself and picked another abusive man to spend my life with. He was just as bad as Don, just in a different way.

He was loud, aggressive and a know it all who actually knew nothing. When he drank beer he was belligerent, but when he drank liquor he transformed into an out of control, destructive, abusive madman. His drunken rampages landed him in jail several times where he would be held in custody until he sobered up. Eric hated Leo with a passion. Melissa and Conrad tolerated him to a point.

It wasn't long before Leo became physically abusive to me and my children. Leo put my children down, swore at them, and grounded them unnecessarily. Leo made fun of the way Eric spoke. He teased him about his appearance, and he called him a little pussy to his face. More than once he would drag Eric out of bed and would often push and shove him around. It wasn't just Eric though, he punched Conrad one day for not saying "excuse me" loud enough after burping. Leo once kicked Melissa in the shin when she was a little girl. Leo manhandled me all the time. One time he pushed me so hard it caused me to fall and cut the back of my head open. He often would grab me forcibly and not let me go and scream in my face. On one occasion when I had pneumonia he wrapped his arms around me from behind across my chest and kept squeezing me like a boa constrictor until I could hardly breath anymore. I managed to get out the words, "I can't breathe" and Leo said, "Then die." Just like Eric's father, Leo controlled all the money. Like many abused women I got out of one horribly abusive situation and right into another one.

Eric hated living with Leo. He was constantly in his room to avoid being tortured and belittled by him. He was like a prisoner in his own home. Eric didn't like participating in any family events because of Leo's presence. He went through the motions at birthdays, holidays, and Christmas, but his heart wasn't in it. He was nervous and uncomfortable being around Leo, and he hardly ever spoke to him. I could see Eric was miserable.

When Eric was fourteen I gave birth to his brother Leo Jr. Things were worse than ever at home. The children loved to spend weekends at their grandmother Yourkin's place as they couldn't wait to get away from Leo Sr., Eric more than the others as things between him and Leo Sr. kept getting worse.

As Eric's sixteenth birthday approached, he began to make a show of packing all his belongings, preparing to leave. He told me that he was planning to move in with my mother when he turned sixteen. I gave birth to his sister Leeanna right before his birthday. I didn't want Eric to leave, but I knew how unhappy he was at home, so I didn't fight it. Looking back, I should have taken all the children and moved too. I should have stuck with my son, but I was still struggling mightily with my own demons and was afraid of what might happen if I did. I had no confidence in myself at all.

Eric and I were close and were always able to talk to each other in ways that many mothers and sons can't. Eric tried to help me get out of the situation I was in with Leo Sr. He was smarter than I was in many ways. He told me to just leave Leo Sr. and go it on my own. He didn't know why I couldn't do what he did. The only reason that he was leaving was because of Leo Sr. so he tried to convince me to do so myself. He was worried about his siblings' safety and my safety.

I was going through the same patterns of abuse that I had experienced in my previous relationship with Don. I was a weak, damaged fool. I should have listened to Eric back then as he had more common sense than I did. When Eric turned sixteen he carried out his plan, and he left and moved to my mother's place in Bethany, Ontario. I was heartbroken, but I knew he would be happier there. It was awful seeing how miserable he was around Leo Sr. I missed Eric so much. I went to Bethany and visited Eric as often as I could, and we wrote each other letters quite often. My mother didn't have a house phone nor did either of them have a cell phone at the time. They used my father's phone (he lived about 5 kilometers away) or the pay phone on the main road of the little hamlet near where they lived. Eric would call me as often as he could.

Eric enrolled in a high school near Lindsay, Ontario; he was bused there every day. Bethany is a very small place, there was not much to do there, and as Eric was a teenager, he wanted more than just to sit around in a small town while living with his grandmother, and for obvious reasons he had never been a big fan of school. He started skipping school to hang out in Lindsay with his friends. The school notified us about this, and he was spoken to. I stressed to Eric how important it was for him to attend school, get his credits, and graduate with a diploma. It fell on deaf ears. Eric continued skipping school. Then one day when he was seventeen, he ran away from my mother's place. She called me and frantically told me that Eric was gone, and she didn't know where he was. I was panic stricken. I immediately headed up to Bethany to find him. All sorts of things were running through my mind; my anxiety was going through the roof. Even though he was seventeen, and he wasn't with me anymore, he was still my baby.

Luka at his Eminem Stage

I arrived at my mother's place and got the details of what had happened. My mother told me that Eric must have climbed out his bedroom window. I checked through Eric's room and some of his clothes and belongings were missing. Where the hell would he go? I went over to my father's place to see if he had heard from Eric. He told me he had seen him earlier that day when he was driving home. Eric told my dad he was going for a walk. I phoned Eric's school to fill them in on what was going on and to see if by chance they had heard anything. They told me that Eric had phoned into the school and told them that he was taking a leave of absence. I told the principal I was coming right over to the school to speak with her.

When I arrived at the school the principal filled me in on what she knew. She said Eric and a friend had called to let her know they were both taking a leave of absence from school, and they would make sure that they returned their text books. The other student had run away from home as well. I was very relieved that the principal had heard from Eric, but I also was quite shocked for two reasons, that Eric had pulled this stunt and that he was responsible because he had phoned the school to let them know his intentions. I asked the principal if the school phone had a call log and she said yes. I asked to see the number Eric had called her from. It was a Toronto number. I then asked the principal if I could use her phone and call it back. When she said that I could, I redialed the number. It rang a few times then a man answered. It was Eric's father. I said, "Put Eric on the phone!" Eric came on the line and said, "Oh hi, I was going to call you. How did you know where I was?" I said, "I tracked you down; I'm at your school." I asked Eric what the hell he was doing? I was so confused. I couldn't believe he was at his father's place as Eric hardly ever associated with his dad.

He said he and his friend decided neither one of them liked living in a small town, and that they wanted more, so they decided to take a break from school and move to Toronto. Eric went on to say that they had both hitch hiked from Omemee, where his friend lived, to Bowmanville, and that's where Eric's dad picked them both up. They were both going to live at Eric's father's place for a while. I was flabbergasted!

I composed myself and expressed to Eric how worried we all were that he had run away like this and that we were all terribly concerned about him because we had no idea where he was. Eric apologized and said he intended to call me and let me know that he was okay and what his plans were. He just hadn't gotten around to doing it yet.

I was so angry at Don for not being a responsible parent. The least he could have done was contact Eric's school and ask them to notify me that Eric was with him. I asked Eric why he was at his dad's. I thought he didn't even like him, they never got along. Eric said he and his dad were going to try to have a better relationship. His father was remarried, and Eric had met his new wife a few times, and he liked her. Both Don and his new wife had been diagnosed with mental illnesses. I was not comfortable with Eric's choice at all. I asked him to reconsider his decision and move back to his grandmother's place, finish high school, and take it from there. If he still wanted to move back to the city, he would be in a better position to do so with a high school degree. I even offered him to come back home with me if he wanted to, but that was out of the question because of Leo Sr.

Despite all of my protests, Eric decided he was going to stay with his father. Of course, things did not go well for Eric while he was living there. His father let him drink alcohol and allowed him to drive his pickup truck when he had been drinking, and without a license. Eric and his friend would drive the truck all over the place; they would even frequently drive down to my house to see me. I repeatedly called the police to report that my son was driving without a license and that sometimes he was under the influence of alcohol as well. I did this until the police were finally able to catch Eric behind the wheel and charge him for driving without a license. Don was cautioned by the police not to give Eric the keys to his vehicle again. Eric was extremely upset that he got charged and that he got into trouble with the police. I never confessed to him that it was I who called the police on him, although that confession finally came out while I was being interrogated by the Montreal police during the murder investigation in 2012. I was trying to prevent Eric from getting into serious trouble. I was terrified that he was going to get into a car accident. Eric was so young. I didn't want him to start out on his own in life that way; I wanted Eric to make good choices. It made me furious that Don had been so irresponsible and stupid.

Eric and his friend eventually had a falling out and parted ways. Eric stayed with his father for a while longer, but things were not working out between them, which of course was no surprise to me, so Eric moved out. Eric went to live with my brother Greg for a short time, but they didn't get along either, so Eric moved to Lindsay, Ontario, to live in an assisted living group home. Eric did not like living in the Lindsay group home either. The other residents of the group home were there for various mental health issues, and this made Eric feel very uncomfortable. I visited Eric there, and he didn't seem happy at all, so we would often go out shopping or to lunch so I could take his mind off things. Eric was on some prescribed medication at the time, and he was not in a very good head space.

One day he called me on the phone from the group home. Right away it was obvious something was off. He was rambling on about Marilyn Monroe, and he told me he wasn't feeling right. He sounded very medicated: his voice was slurred, and he sounded so far away. He told me he thought he had taken too many pills. My heart sank, I was all the way in Toronto and there was nothing I could do. I told him to stay put, and I would call him right back. I phoned the group home coordinator and told him Eric was in trouble and asked if he could please get over there and help him. When I called Eric back another resident of the home answered the phone and told me Eric had left. I called the police, but they had already picked him up. Eric was trying to walk to the hospital a few blocks away, and the police happened upon him and noticed he was in distress and took him into the hospital. Eric asked the emergency room nurse to call me. He was still quite out of it, but stable. The nurse put Eric on the phone with me, and we talked for a few minutes. I was so thankful that he was all right, but I was terribly concerned and upset. I never really got a straight answer as to why, or how this happened.

Not long after that Eric decided that he wanted to move out of the assisted living home and back to Toronto. He found a nice apartment a few blocks away from where I was living. I helped him move in. He was receiving ODSP at the time, which is a government assistance program in Canada.

I was glad that we were living so close to each other. We got to see each other every day. Eric would walk down to see me, or I would drive up to see him. We would go places together all the time. One day while I was over visiting Eric, I discovered some empty liquor bottles and wine glasses. This was very concerning for me, and I discussed this problem with Eric on more than one occasion. Eric was not eating properly either, so I began bringing over home cooked meals, so he would have something healthy to eat. He down played it saying he was a social drinker, but I knew otherwise. I suspected he was drinking because he was depressed.

It was around this time that Eric started working on a new look. He dyed his hair blond, and he started wearing track suits and long chain necklaces. He had kind of an Eminem thing going on. Eric had started to pursue a dream of his, which was becoming a model, and it seemed to be working out for him. He was getting some work. He had the look that people were after, and he soon began to get lots of modelling jobs and was making a good amount of money, and his self-confidence was soaring. This all made me happy as he had been picked on so much as a child.

He wound up moving in with two friends of his who were brothers. They came from a wealthy family, and they offered Eric to move into their condo with them. Eric started seeing a girl. They were dating but nothing serious, she was a mutual friend of all of them. The brothers were two conniving opportunists, and the two of them took advantage of Eric and the girl he was dating big time. She also came from a very wealthy family and she had lots of credit cards with huge limits. The brothers came up with a scheme, and the two of them smooth talked Eric and his new girlfriend into executing it. They got her to run up her credit cards purchasing expensive items for them. Eric's only role in the scheme was being present with her while she was shopping for the items. The brothers took the stuff and hoarded it away. They were probably planning to re-sell it. Her father was a business man in Woodbridge, Ontario, and when he got wind that his daughter's credit cards were rapidly being maxed out, he got furious and stepped in. He banned her from seeing any of them including Eric, and he notified the police about what was going on. The police investigated and, in the end, Eric was the fall guy who was charged with fraud.

I had no idea all this had been going on. I had moved to Peterborough and was not in touch with Eric as much as usual. Prior to the police involvement, Eric and I had made plans to meet in Toronto for a visit. I showed up in Toronto on my scheduled visit day and waited at the plaza for Eric as planned. He never showed up. I called his cell phone several times but there was no answer. He never stood me up; he was always on time; he looked forward to our visits. I waited at the plaza for him for about an hour and half; he was a no show. I was becoming extremely concerned.

I headed back to Peterborough worried sick. I repeatedly called Eric all that evening and the following morning. Nothing. I decided if I didn't hear from Eric by that afternoon, I was going to call the police and file a missing person's report. An hour or so later Eric called me collect on my house phone from jail. He explained to me what had happened and what he had been charged with, and he told me that he was being detained at Maplehurst Institution in Milton, Ontario. I was in shock! He asked me to help him get a legal aid certificate and get him a bail hearing. I got right on it, and I also phoned Eric's psychiatrist to fill him in on the situation. We got the legal aid certificate, retained a lawyer, got a letter from Eric's psychiatrist, and we got a bail hearing date. Eric asked me to be a co-surety with one of the brothers he was living with. Eric didn't want to live with me because he hated Leo Sr. At this point the brothers were claiming they wanted to help their poor friend Eric, one of them saying he wanted to help me bail Eric out and even wanted Eric to still live with them. I agreed to be Eric's surety, and I made it very clear to Eric that in light of the circumstances, I did not trust either of the brothers.

Eric spent about two weeks in custody awaiting his bail hearing, which felt like forever. The court date finally came, and I headed down to Toronto for the bail hearing with $2000 cash, which is what I was told the court would be asking for bail. I had never been a surety for anyone, and I had no idea how the process went. The $2000 I had was for first and last month's rent on a nicer house I was going to rent in Peterborough. It didn't matter, I needed to get my son out of jail and straighten out this mess.

The Justice of the Peace said that Eric would have to live with me as one of his bail conditions. I explained the situation that had to do with him and Leo Sr. to the Justice of the Peace, and I asked him if Eric could live with my mother, and thankfully he said yes. Eventually Eric was brought in with his hands cuffed in front of him and put in the prisoner's box in the courtroom. The judge spoke to Eric and addressed the charges and the conditions he would have to follow if he was released on bail. Then the judge spoke to me about my responsibilities as a surety. The judge was satisfied that we both understood our roles and responsibilities, and Eric was granted bail. The courthouse closed by this time, but I was permitted to wait inside for Eric to be processed and released. As soon as he came through the door, we wrapped our arms around each other and hugged, I was so happy to have my son out of jail, and Eric was so grateful that I had gotten him out. I remember thinking at the time that he seemed to have learned so much from this experience, and neither of us would ever have to be in this situation again.

Eric and I attended the court again at a later date for his sentencing hearing. Eric received a nine-month conditional sentence and probation. Eric did all he was supposed to do during this time. He resided with my mother, attended every meeting with his probation officer, finished his community service hours, and he did not associate with any of the people who involved him in this mess. Eric made good choices and successfully completed all his probation conditions, I was very proud of him. After Eric's probation was over he no longer had to live with my mother, so he moved back to Toronto.

That year Eric got a hair transplant, although there have been rumors of him having a lot of plastic surgery, this is the one and only cosmetic surgery I know of and can confirm. Eric moved around quite a bit, so it's very hard for me to remember every single place he lived, although I do remember that the apartments I did go to visit him in were always very nice, clean, high end, and beautifully decorated. He started being an escort around this time, and he continued to do a lot of modelling. He was making fantastic money, he had a nice vehicle, expensive clothes, shoes, and sunglasses. He looked amazing. It seemed like he was finally becoming confident and growing into his true self. Of course I worried, but all I wanted was for him to be happy, and it seemed like he was finally on his way there.

Anna and Luka at one of his apartments

Eric is very kind and generous; he always has been. When he was making a lot of cash, he would give all of us in his family money and buy us gifts all the time. Eric and I loved to spend our birthdays together, as we're both born in July. In 2005 we celebrated our birthdays in Toronto at the Canadian National Exhibition, Ontario Place. We went for a helicopter ride over the city and had dinner at the Hard Rock Café. We had a fabulous day. That year he bought me a lovely marble kitchen set as well. Eric loved to travel and with his newfound financial stability he started travelling all over the world. He took trips to New York, California, Denver, Europe, Switzerland, and Russia and many more places. In 2006 Eric wanted to do something bigger for our birthdays than we had done the previous year, so he booked a trip for us to go to Montreal together. We travelled there by train, stayed in a beautiful hotel, shopped, took lots of photos, and did a lot of sightseeing. We went to the theatre, cafes, and dined in fine restaurants. We had an amazing time.

Around this time Eric legally changed his name to Luka Rocco Magnotta. He did this to give himself a fresh start in life as there were a lot of painful memories attached to the name Eric Newman, and since he was aspiring to be a model, it wasn't that odd of a decision to me.

Luka's career as a model/escort acquainted him with many unusual people. Although I was glad he seemed happy, I worried about him and his lifestyle all the time. Some of his clients were in positions of power and authority, some were public figures, some were affiliated with organized crime, some were cruel, and some had strange and bizarre fetishes. Luka was becoming exposed to a very dangerous, undesirable lifestyle. Luka began telling me that he was receiving threats and was stalked at times by some of his weird clientele. Luka started acting paranoid and very fearful for his safety. I think the repercussions of associating with these individuals played a big role in Luka's decision to frequently move because of his safety concerns. I suspected that Luka was not seeing his psychiatrist regularly, and I don't think he was taking any prescribed medication either. In early 2007 Luka declared bankruptcy. I knew of this, but I don't know a lot of the details.

That same year Luka booked a very elaborate trip for the two of us to celebrate our birthdays together once again, this time he was taking us to the Bahamas. We flew to Nassau and stayed in a high-class hotel on Paradise Island. We took boat trips, spent a lot of time shopping, took lots of photos, we jet skied together, lounged on the beach, we experienced the island culture, and enjoyed the fabulous island entertainment in the evenings. As a grand finale to our trip, Luka rented a white, stretch limo to take us back to the airport. It was an incredible birthday trip. I always appreciated everything

Luka did for me, and I love him for being so good to me; he is a very generous person, but it didn't matter where I was with Luka, we always had a wonderful time together. I miss that; I miss my son.

At one point rumors began to surface that Luka was in a relationship with Karla Holmolka. She was a Canadian serial killer who, with her first husband Paul Bernardo, raped and murdered at least three minors. Bernardo was the mastermind of the situation, and while he remained in prison, Karla was convicted, served her time, and was released from prison.

Some say Luka started the rumors himself but after doing countless hours of online investigating, I believe that an online forum group were the ones that started it. One group has a very unstable administrator who is obsessed with Karla and basically stalks her. Luka had a heavy Internet presence at the time. He was trying to make it big as a model; he had tons of photos of himself out there-models do that. The administrator of the Watching Karla Holmolka Group began stalking and harassing Luka as well as Karla. In my opinion she trumped up these rumors of Luka's involvement with Karla to bring attention to the forum group. I've learned through the police investigation that Luka had many online identities, so what? This is not uncommon. Many people have them for various reasons. This only became heavily scrutinized because a crime took place.

Around the same time Luka became involved in a serious relationship with a man. Unfortunately this was an unhealthy relationship from the get go, and it really took its toll on Luka. His new boyfriend was from a wealthy and "connected" family. He was good looking and he had a great career, but he had problems, big ones. He lived a double life. With his family and friends he was the successful, decent, macho straight guy, and with Luka he was the gay and sexually promiscuous guy with a kinky side. Luka and he were in a serious relationship, and Luka thought they were in love. Luka wanted his new boyfriend to come clean and come out to his family and friends about his sexual orientation and tell them he was gay, and he was in a relationship with Luka. Luka told him to stop living in denial and trying to juggle two lives. But he made every excuse in the book why he couldn't tell his family and friends, or he would agree to do so and then not follow through with it. This posed a huge issue in their relationship, and they fought over it all the time. It upset Luka terribly, it made him feel unworthy and frustrated. Luka had stopped escorting and was faithful because he was in a committed relationship.

His boyfriend on the other hand was not faithful to Luka. He had an insatiable sex addiction. He would frequent bath houses in downtown Toronto and have sex with multiple men on a regular basis. He would also hook up with random men on Craigslist and have sex with them too. Not only would he not come clean to his family and friends and bring his relationship out in the open, he whored around on Luka every day. Luka confided in me about this, and it made me sick. I could not believe that someone could be this insensitive and cruel to my son. I had many long, heated conversations with this man about his behavior toward Luka. I would talk to him for hours sometimes trying to convince him to stop living in denial and be honest with his mother and seek help for his sex addiction. He told me he was in therapy, but it wasn't working. Luka couldn't take it anymore, and he broke up with him. He harassed and plagued Luka relentlessly for quite some time, but Luka refused to lower his standards and take him back if he wasn't willing to change his ways. My son deserved better.

4

LUKA

I actually think society is extremely sick—Luka Magnotta

In my interviews with Luka one thing was obvious. He doesn't like talking about the video, or the actual act itself. It makes him very uncomfortable. But he wanted to make some other points very clear.

He is not crazy, and he didn't want to use the NCR defense.

At the time of my trial, I wished strongly to testify and defend myself. I wanted to speak. At the advice of ineffective counsel, I reluctantly declined and was told the insanity defense was the only way. I wanted absolutely nothing to do with this absurd defense. I was urged to meet with psychiatrists and doctors. I wanted no part of this absurd circus. These doctors presented me with absurd theories and accusations. I denied them all then my team insisted I agree and admit to the most bizarre and craziest claims made against me in order to be successful with the insanity defense.

It infuriated me when Luc LeClair wouldn't let up on the insanity defense. We argued constantly and screamed at one another. Every time a weird claim was listed off to me, I was pushed to admit it because it will help my case. So unprofessional. I considered contacting the bar association or the college of physicians, but they insisted they know best.

A certain doctor was constantly asking me if he would be "chosen" it was bordering on begging. It reminded me of a child on the way to the ice cream shop. "Am I going to be chosen" constantly. "I'm on your side, my report is what your lawyer wants."

This was Dr. Joel Watts of course. He was and is obsessed with making a name for himself. He guided me in the direction he wanted in order to gain the diagnosis he wanted. Even when I told him I was not schizophrenic, he pushed the evaluation report just like he pushed to join the police on the plane to Germany to pick me up. He included himself in every step of the process, just like he does when he writes about me and appears in interviews and lies about me. I am not schizophrenic and neither is my father. We went along with this because of our renegade doctors and lawyers.

He would say, "I feel you're fighting this diagnosis and trying to deny your true self." I told him to fuck off, and I was tired of having this ridiculous defense shoved down my throat.

I never asserted my position that I was fine and completely 100 percent stable. It is not within my capacity as a person to fool or outsmart forensic psychiatrists or skilled attorneys. The pushback now, unfortunately, will be that I manipulated these professionals. That is purely revolting. Of course they won't admit to pushing their agenda. I exposed their hoax. Perhaps they should think twice about not allowing defendants to speak the truth and tell all the facts. It's egregious. The idiots in the media have a long history of twisting long stories and will try and twist this too. No, the reader should pay attention to the facts and not allow themselves to be bombarded with sensationalist reporting.

Dr. Watts cannot sit with a straight face any longer and defame my character as he's done. It is disgraceful and I feel used. My message to Joel Watts is, no one believes your twisted reports, no one believes the story you have pushed, and people are tired of hearing your attention seeking interviews and reading your self serving books. What you say about me is not true and the blame is on you for being *complicit with others to thrust forward this horrendous defense.*

He didn't kill any kittens.

I never harmed any animals. I actually adore and love them. I take care of animals nowadays. Manny Lopez and John Carpenter, two psychopaths who abused me severely, need to be looked at. They know the things they are responsible for. Members from PETA sent me death threats.

In 2009 I was on vacation in Miami when John the Carpenter and Manny Lopez physically abused me. The police did nothing.

When people accuse me of being involved in animal cruelty videos, I wonder where the proof is. My face is definitely not shown, I know that since I am not involved. My lawyer and I believe I was set up. Photos of me were photoshopped, and this entire thing has to do with Manny Lopez and his desire to make money in illegal markets on the dark web. I am not concerned in any way about this ridiculous story and could care less.

He doesn't care about fame.

I am frequently being portrayed as this fame-starved unstable person. This inaccurate spin could not be further from the truth. This label is getting old. The truth is I have never requested or participated in any interview with any media outlets in the last seven years. Hardly the act of someone addicted to attention.

People have claimed incredible lies about me. It's unbelievable that any credible news outlet would publish such lies. I am told that a lot of irrelevant weirdos have claimed to be in relationships with me or to have befriended me or formed some nonexistent connection. I do not know any of these idiots, nor have I ever heard of them. I don't even know what they look like. I just continue to laugh at these irrelevant attention seekers.

He is doing great.

I've learned you never know how strong you are until being strong is the only option you have. I've learned to trust nobody. I've learned the media do not report facts and most of the time its self-serving opinions. I've learned in the last six years not to retreat but to always reload. As Lincoln has said "whatever you are, make yourself good at it."

I'm outside the majority of the time; I play a lot of videogames. We have movie nights. We all have our own TVs. I have painting class and I exercise a lot. I practice language studies. People need to be proud of their accomplishments. Know your value and share it with everyone.

Manny is real.

Other people's opinions of me mean absolutely nothing. I ignore the noise that other people rant. The people who know me know Manny. So when idiots were not witness to the events and who weren't even there give their opinion, who cares, they are completely irrelevant.

5

VLADIMIR

*Extremely weird and unstable people online have
no lives so they cause mischief*—Luka Magnotta

Police say that Luka has gone by numerous aliases, set up
set up dozens of online usernames and maintained as many
as seventy Facebook pages and twenty websites. It is hard
to know what they mean by "websites" but that is what they
say.

Luka disagrees. *The failing media falsely claimed I had
hundreds of accounts. This was a huge lie perpetrated by
Internet trolls. I had only a couple social media accounts. If
idiots steal my photos and post them that's not my problem. I
was and am too busy living my own life to pay any attention.*

He wanted people to know who he was. There is no
denying that. He would pay people to alter photographs of
him and then post them online, of him doing something that
made him look rich, or look special, maybe he would be
behind the wheel of a sportscar he didn't own, or maybe he
would be traveling to a country he had never been to. He
wrote under numerous different names saying that he was
dating famed Canadian serial killer Karla Homolka, then he
would leave comments under more different names saying
what a violent psychopath Luka Magnotta was. Always in
the third person, always trying to create more buzz.

He used many names online, such as Vladimir, or Jimmy.
He would post about himself under some of these names,
saying of himself such things as "he is in fact now living in
the Caribbean with his new wife Karla Homolka," or that he

is a "master manipulator" Then he would leave all sorts of comments using other accounts saying things like "Man is that Luka Magnotta so fucked up or what?" Always building the buzz, upselling the brand.

At one point he was interviewed about the Homolka rumors by a reporter with the *Toronto Sun* by the name of Joe Warmington who said "He might have been the creepiest person I ever interviewed. You spend ten seconds with him, and you easily come to the conclusion it's all in his own head and all for attention,"

One post that one could find on the Internet a few weeks before the murder was of Luka wearing a purple hoodie holding something that looks like an icepick. It said, "There is apparently a video circulating around the deep web called *One Lunatic One Ice Pick Video*. Does anyone have a copy of it?

In his report Dr. Joel Watts stated that he asked Luka if he put up posts on the Internet that promoted the death of Jun Lin. He says that Luka said "I have been trying to make some sense of it. I hope it was not me. I don't remember doing it; it feels weird."

Watts also said in his report that Luka "falsified his identity at times in order to either boost his self-image or as he alleges, to "scare people" due to years of abuse, humiliation, and an intense need to be recognized, loved and not feel alone or abandoned. His paranoia has also driven him to falsely represent himself. He has withheld information about his symptoms of mental illness due to fears of stigmatization and hospitalization. At times he has denied responsibility for involvement with videos depicting animal abuse due to shame and fear of persecution in addition to fears of prosecution."

Luka says this is all bullshit. *I was living in many different countries and modeled for many years. I lived in Los Angeles, Miami, and New York City. I did runways, photo shoots, and private events. My manager suggested*

I try out for reality shows and I reluctantly did. This is in no way evidence of narcissism as armchair lonely Internet users claim. I tried out for three reality shows. Big fucking deal. Also for my job I had to have photos taken. Idiots who wonder why I have so many photos need to get a life. I had my photos only on my private Internet accounts. The failing media claimed I had hundreds of Internet accounts. This was a huge lie perpetrated by Internet trolls. If idiots steal my photos and post them elsewhere that's not my problem.

I don't feel comfortable talking about the video, but I will say this; I never posted it online. That's a lie. How can anyone prove who posted it online unless they see them do it? Ill-informed armchair Internet detectives assume it was me. In court it was proven it never came from my email or my IP address. Just because someone is involved in something, doesn't mean they started it. As far as being framed I will say this: I haven't decided on an appeal, so I must be careful. People were stalking me, that was proven.

Luka at an early modeling shoot

Dr. Watts said that Luka admitted that he had exaggerated and embellished his reputation on the Internet. Again, lots of us do that, to varying levels. While most of us don't pay people to alter photos to make ourselves look like we are behind the wheel of a sports car like Luka did, many of us attempt to use the Internet constantly to make ourselves look better. If you don't think I am correct go check out Instagram. Look how hot I am, look how popular I am, look at all the friends I have, look at how much fun I am having, look at how perfect my ass is. In today's social media world, vanity is often thought of as a virtue. It's all a matter of degrees, and like with many other things, Magnotta took things much further than most.

As for dating Karla? He told me *I believe the Karla Homolka rumor was started by unstable Internet stalkers who would frequently show up outside my home and places of work.*

But according to the Watts report, Luka admitted he linked himself to Karla Homolka, saying, "Yes, it was stupid. I would try to be other people to protect myself, to seem tougher." Watts says that Luka said it was all about making him appear to be of higher status than he was, that he wanted to be a bit of a celebrity, but he also got off on people being intimidated of him, and that Luka had written stories online anonymously implying that Luka Magnotta was a psychopath. For some reason Luka wanted to be scary. But as much as he tried, he really wasn't. Until the video of the murder came to light, then he actually was.

Again, other people do things like this all the time on the Internet. Look how beautiful I am. How popular. How rich. Look at where I am on vacation. Like other things with Luka, when he tried to do something to make himself fit in, it was just ridiculously off. "Look who is dating a serial killer" just doesn't do it for a lot of people. But it obviously did something for Luka.

There was much on the Internet that made it appear that Luka was a successful model and porn actor who was hounded by the Canadian version of the paparazzi. But when people dug into it more, it appeared all of the information was posted by Luka himself! Twice he attempted to put up a Wikipedia page about himself. Twice they took it down.

At one point Luka was confronted by a journalist named Alex West about the possibility of being the person who killed some kittens in a series of videos. The videos are truly awful, and there is little doubt that Luka is behind them. A group of animal rights vigilantes were making it their mission to track Luka down. They claimed when they figured out who he was, he would taunt them, at times pretending to be other people to try and infiltrate their group. They offered rewards for people who could find him or knew where he was. They tried to trick him into coming to the United States where they would capture him and turn him over to authorities. One plot involved him even meeting Ron Jeremy in an elaborate sting that would involve Luka being offered a job on a porn set.

Luka denied being part of the videos when West was in his face, but soon afterwards West received an email from "John Kilbride," which is the name of one of the victims of the infamous pair of killers, Ian Brady and Myra Hindley. The email said "Once you kill, and taste blood, it's impossible to stop. The urge is just too strong not to continue." It continued: Next time you hear from me it will be in a movie I am producing that will have some humans in it, not just pussys.:) and ended with: "Getting away with all this, now that's genius." It is widely accepted that this email came from Luka.

But Luka told me that *It's very important to include that I don't know who any of these animal activists are. They constantly blab to the press that there was a cat and mouse game going on, or I was taunting them. Or that I emailed them under assumed names. That is completely false. I have no idea who these idiots are. They have some sick obsession with me.*

There is no doubt that Luka loved the power of the Internet. It makes one wonder, if it wasn't for the Internet, would any of this ever have happened at all?

6

ANNA

They were in an SUV with me and I left. Whatever they did after I left is unbeknown to me. I was told they mailed boxes to different places. My handwriting was not on any boxes and my DNA was not on anything—Luka Magnotta

Time passed and Luka returned to escorting and started dating again. As for me, I was going through a very difficult time in my life. My sister had passed away and right around the same time period as this happened we had a traumatic house fire. The last time I physically saw Luka prior to his arrest for alleged murder was in August 2010. We met in Toronto. When Luka showed up he seemed very preoccupied. He was looking around nervously and acting very oddly. He told me that he was very busy and could only stay for a few minutes. He gave everyone who came to see him, which was me, my mother, Melissa, Leo Jr., Leeanna, and his two nephews a hug then he gave me a late birthday card with some money in it, said he had to run and left. The entire visit was all of maybe fifteen minutes. Luka's behavior concerned me, he looked very troubled, like he was afraid of something or someone.

We talked on the phone shortly after that, and I asked him if everything was okay as he seemed so disjointed and nervous. Luka told me that he was freaked out, that he was scared. People were following him, and he was being stalked, and he told me that he had even reported it to the police. I was very worried about him, and I feared for his safety.

Around the end of 2010 beginning of 2011, rumors began circulating in the family that there was a video posted online of Luka killing kittens. I did not want to hear about it, and I did not believe it. I knew Luka couldn't do something like this. It was too bizarre to even think about.

One family member even sent me a private Facebook message with a link to this supposed video and asked me what the hell was going on. I clicked on the link, and the site said the video

had been removed, and I didn't investigate it further. I was very confused, and I did not want to believe this to be true. I didn't even want to search into it and find out what was going on. I just didn't want to know.

I knew that Luka was in contact with a lawyer in Manhattan by the name of Romeo Salta, but I wasn't sure why. I later learned that Luka had been confiding in Mr. Salta about his fears and safety concerns. He informed Mr. Salta that he had been beaten up, and he even sent him a photo showing his injuries. Luka was also seeking advice from Mr. Salta about the allegations being made against him regarding the online cat killing videos. The videos got the attention of animal rights activists/stalkers who were determined to find Luka and get justice for this alleged crime. Luka gave me Romeo Salta's contact information and told me to contact Mr. Salta if something should ever happen to him, Luka also gave my contact information to Mr. Salta. I was becoming increasing concerned about Luka. It seemed Luka was terrified of someone or something, and if he had been involved in such a horrible thing with the cats, it was a huge sign that something very wrong was happening.

In January 2011 I received a call from an unfamiliar number. It was a medical professional calling from the Mount Sinai Medical Centre in Miami Beach, Florida. I was informed that Luka was brought into their emergency department by the police. Luka had told the police that he had been taken to Miami against his will; he had been raped; he was confused, disoriented, sunburned, and he was terrified. Luka asked the hospital to call me. He wanted me to vouch for him as he wanted to be released. I felt sick when I found out that Luka had claimed he was raped and felt that he needed to be in a hospital. I refused to vouch for his release. I felt it was imperative that Luka stay in the hospital for observation and get some medical help. Luka ended up staying at the hospital for a very short time under observation then he was let go. I later learned that Luka's father and a friend of Luka's vouched for his release.

Luka in the Bahamas

The whole situation upset me a great deal. The medical professionals at the Miami hospital could obviously see that Luka was in a crisis and desperately needed help. Why were they phoning his family and friends in Canada to vouch for his release? We are not qualified to make a medical decision like that, especially from so far away. It was their call. There was no way for them to even verify who we were over the phone. Why not try to contact his doctor or psychiatrist? What purpose did it serve for the hospital to call anyone if one parent (me) said don't release him, and the other parent (his father) and Luka's friend said release him? Luka was twenty-eight years old at the time, and this was the first time a mental health care professional had involved me in any sort of decision making regarding my adult son. I was glad they had asked for my input, and I felt confident that they were going to do the right thing for Luka. I was sadly mistaken. In my opinion Luka was released from that hospital way too soon, they should have investigated and documented the abuse Luka had been repeatedly saying was happening to him, and the police should have started an investigation.

When Luka returned to Canada, it was obvious that he was still in a very unwell state of mind. He was furious with me that I didn't vouch for his release from the Miami hospital. He told me off; he said that he didn't want to speak to me again. This was very out of character for Luka, for we were always close, and he was always very respectful to me. Even though Luka stopped speaking to me, he remained in contact with my mother and Melissa, and he would ask about me, wondering how I was. During our estrangement I found out through my mother and Melissa that Luka told them that he was living in Russia and that he had gotten married to a Russian woman. Luka told my mother that he was extremely happy with his new wife and his new life. I was blown away when she told me this. I did not believe a word of it. Luka was not in a good head space, and I knew he was making it all up, but why?

By the beginning of 2012, Luka was speaking to me again, and he sent me some photos of himself via email. There was a drastic change in his appearance. He had a very different look about him. I was used to him changing up his look and style a bit for modelling but never anything like this. This was even more shocking than when he dyed his hair blond when he was a teenager. In the photos, Luka's hair was long, and his eyes looked vacant. One photo was particularly shocking to me. In this photo Luka was extremely pale; his eyes looked black; he looked thinner than usual, and he looked much younger, like a teenage boy.

He looked very unwell. It was very difficult for me to look at those photos.

After a while our estrangement ended and Luka began to talk to me again. Luka called me up one evening, and we were just chatting about everyday stuff, and then out of the blue, he brought up the cat killing videos. I was speechless, shocked, and extremely uncomfortable. He started by asking me if I had heard anything about him killing cats in some videos. I really didn't know how to respond. I didn't want to believe it was true, and I never, ever expected to be having a conversation about it with Luka. He went on to tell me that people were saying horrible things about him on the Internet, people were looking for him and animal rights activists were threatening him and coming after him. After he finished talking I mustered up the nerve to say, "Yes, I did hear about it, is it true?" Luka said, "Go on your Internet for yourself and see" and he instructed me how to search for the cat killing video. When I found the site with the video, Luka said, "Play it." I hit play and immediately I was shocked. There was a man that looked like Luka on a bed with kittens. I stopped the video, I didn't want to watch anymore of it.

I said, "Did you kill those kittens?!" Luka said he was forced to do it by a horrible man named Manny. He said Manny threatened to harm him if he didn't comply. Luka also told me Manny had abused him in the past, and Manny was the one who took him to Miami and raped him. I was hysterical. I said, we need to call the police. Luka said, if I called the police that I would never see him again. He sounded terrified. I tried to reason with him, but he was adamant, No police! I was feeling physically ill. I didn't know what more I could say to Luka or what to do. I was afraid to do anything as I didn't want to lose Luka or put his life in jeopardy at the hands of Manny.

Luka called me again a week or so later and changed his story. He said it wasn't him in the cat killing videos. It was someone named 'Jack' who looked like him. He asked me to go back on the computer and look at a particular frame of the video. He instructed me to click the cursor to a certain time on the video and hit play then freeze the video, so I did and in that video frame there was an image of a man who looked like Luka to me, and I told him so. I was so confused. Luka said someone was trying to frame him. I knew it was Manny.

People in our family were constantly talking about the videos and what was being said online about them, and we were all becoming increasingly concerned for Luka. PETA (People for the Ethical Treatment of Animals) were even contacting family members on line and asking them questions about Luka, trying to get personal information about him, wondering where he might be located. Then I found out that the police were involved. They were looking for Luka too. This was really getting bad; I was frantic.

Another family member and I decided we needed to talk to the police. I spoke with a detective from the Toronto Police Service. The detective informed me that he had watched the cat killing videos, and they disturbed him greatly; then he told me that this sort of behavior can quickly escalate from killing animals to killing people. I was terrified. I told the detective everything I knew, and I fully cooperated with him to help him find Luka, even if it meant that he would be arrested to straighten out this horrible mess. I wanted Luka to be able to tell the police his side of the story about Manny and get some help. I wanted to save Luka before something terrible happened to him or someone else. I told the detective I thought Luka wasn't telling the truth about being in Russia, and I believed he was living in Montreal because he had sent me a card and lottery ticket from there. The detective didn't seem interested in my idea to try and track Luka down through the post mark on the card or locating the terminal the lottery ticket was purchased from. That still bothers me. The detective did, however, ensure me that he would be in contact with the Montreal police.

The next time Luka called me I didn't tell him that I was in contact with the police, but I decided I was going to call Luka out on everything. I started the conversation off by saying, "I have some things I need to say to you, and you are probably not going to like what I've got to say, and maybe you won't want to talk to me again after you hear what they are, but I have got to say them. Luka said, "You can say whatever is on your mind to me, and I will still speak to you, don't worry, just say it."

I started off by saying, "I think you are lying to me. That was you in the cat killing video not someone named "Jack." Then I said, "I don't think you are married and living in Russia." Luka said," What makes you think this?" I said," Nothing is adding up! I saw you in the video with my own two eyes; you sent me a card that was post marked in Montreal." Luka said he had a friend of his in Montreal send the card to me for him. I said, "You're lying, it's your handwriting, stop lying and tell me the truth. This is getting way out of hand!"

He listened quietly as I continued. "I said, Eric you need help. Please let me come to Montreal and pick you up and bring you home and get you some help." I went on to say, "You need to contact the police and talk to them, tell them your side of the story and tell them everything Manny has done to you! You need to deal with this before it gets worse. Luka said in a shocked, kind, soft voice, "I'm sorry you feel this way. Let's agree to disagree, and I am not mad at you."

I was so frustrated. We said goodnight and that we loved each other. I honestly thought I wouldn't hear from Luka again for a while after I had confronted him like that, but the following morning bright and early, he called me to say hi, and he said he was going to the park to feed the pigeons and he loved me very much. I asked him when we could see each other again. He said he was planning to come to Montreal in the late spring or early summer, and we would meet somewhere and visit each other then. I told him I couldn't wait to see him, and I told him I loved him very much, too, and all I wanted to do was help him. I asked him to really think about what I had said to him the night before. I was so relieved that Luka had agreed to meet me in a couple of months.

I spoke with the Toronto detective again and told him Luka and I were going to meet somewhere in Montreal for a visit in a couple of months. I told him I would let him know when and where we would be meeting. All I asked was that the police not tell Luka it was me who gave them this information, he agreed. This gave me some peace of mind knowing that Luka was going to get help very soon, and they could get to the bottom of this this and find Manny. I continued to talk to Luka on the phone regularly, and I kept reminding him about our visit and telling him how much I was looking forward to seeing him. I truly was looking forward to seeing him, hugging him, and doing something, anything, to protect him. I didn't want things to escalate and something terrible to happen. I would have stayed in Montreal until Luka, the police, and I could get to the bottom of this.

In April of 2012 Luka told me he was going to move to California in the spring to start a new life. He said he was going to be acting or modelling there. He seemed quite confident it would work out for him. Luka reassured me that he would still come back to Canada and meet me in Montreal for a visit. I was so relieved. Luka moved and travelled a lot; this was not out of the ordinary for me to hear. We continued to talk on the phone regularly. Luka had days when he seemed okay; then he would have days when he seemed very off. At times he sounded very sad and lonely and at times he sounded agitated, afraid, and preoccupied with his own thoughts. I was hopeful that the move to California would help Luka start fresh and he could escape from Manny. I knew that something had to change.

7

LUKA

I don't give interviews since being in prison. I don't
trust the media at all and have been completely defamed
and slandered for years. The lies they've told are
horrendous and very troubling. It's important to me
that my story be told accurately and without any of
the lies the media tell. Everyone has had their chance
to speak, the lawyers, jury, judge, prosecutor, police,
media, and so on. Now it's my turn—Luka Magnotta

From the Watts Report: "Video number 11 shows assorted
videos from the surveillance cameras at 5720 DeCarie
beginning on May 24th at around 21:30 until May 26th,
2012 at 17:14 when Mr. Magnotta left for the final time with
luggage and wearing sunglasses. His various comings and
goings during this time period can be summarized as the
following: After leaving the apartment at 21:32 on May 24th,
wearing a white t-shirt and long hair, Mr. Magnotta returns
with Mr. Lin at about 20:00. They are recorded entering
the lobby and front hallway. At 02:06 May 25th, 2012, Mr.
Magnotta is seen leaving the building wearing the same
yellow t-shirt that Mr. Lin had been wearing previously. Mr.
Magnotta returns to the apartment about seven minutes later
and is seen checking himself in the mirror in the lobby. He
plays with his hair and looks at himself from side to side.
At 02:47 in the morning, he is seen placing garbage bags in
a garbage container. He is again seen putting more garbage
bags in the garbage drums at 02:52. At 04:02, he returns
more garbage and puts a box in the recycling bin. He seems

to hesitate at one point. At 04:09, he throws out four bottles of wine. At 04:22, he is seen throwing out two pillows with no visible stains. At 04:26, he is seen throwing out more garbage. At 04:31, he places a black garbage bag underneath other garbage in a careful manner. He goes into what appears to be a bathroom to the side of the garbage area and looks at himself in the mirror. At 04:36, he is seen leaving through the front lobby with a black and white puppy in his arms, still wearing the yellow t-shirt, and returns one minute later with the puppy. At 06:07, a man is observed emptying the two garbage drums in the building."

"At 07:43 on May 25th Magnotta leaves the building wearing a pink t-shirt and Mr. Lin's ball cap and he stops to look at himself in the lobby mirror from the side. At 08:48, he returns to the building with a large grey suitcase that appears to be the one the victim's torso was found in. At 09:08, he leaves the building wearing a striped tank top and again checks himself out in the mirror. At 09:09, he returns and leaves again at 09:10. At 12:12, he returns with a plastic bag containing some objects. At 13:09, he is seen throwing out picture frames and wearing blue gloves in the garbage area. At 13:32, he leaves the building through the front door, checks his mailbox but does not look at himself in the mirror (another woman is also present in the lobby)."

"At 14:17, he returns with a plastic bag in his hand. At 15:50, he is seen throwing out more garbage, wearing blue gloves, wearing a striped tank top and Mr. Lin's ball cap. His hair is now for the first time short. He is again seen at 17:12 throwing out clothes, wearing a white t-shirt and sunglasses. At 18:51, he leaves the building with a shoulder bag, a white t-shirt and is again wearing long hair. He glances at himself briefly in the mirror. At 19:29, he returns and his bag is empty. At 21:00, he leaves the building with two large black bags, wearing a white t-shirt, Mr. Lin's ball cap and his hair is short. He returns about two minutes later without any bags. At 21:53, he throws out more clothing, wearing a white t-shirt, ball cap and short hair. At 22:14, he leaves the building with the grey suitcase that appears to contain a heavy object, wearing a white t-shirt, ball cap and short hair. At 22:16, he returns through the front lobby without the suitcase."

"At 05:27 on May 26th, 2012, Magnotta is seen leaving wearing a dark green t-shirt, short hair and Mr. Lin's ball cap through the front lobby. He returns one minute later and then leaves again with two black bags that appear to have heavy contents two minutes following this. He glances at himself briefly in the mirror in the lobby. He returns three minutes later without the bags. At 05:39, he throws out some garbage and again at 05:47. He does the same at 06:26, this time wearing long hair again. At 06:34, he leaves the building through the front lobby with long hair and a shoulder bag, glancing at himself at the mirror. At 09:23, he returns. At 11:11, he is seen leaving with a garbage bag, wearing long hair and again looks at himself in the mirror. At 16:35, he returns without the garbage bag. He is seen again returning to the building at 16:46. At 16:48, he is seen placing two garbage bags in the garbage drums of the building wearing a black t-shirt and same hair. At 17:10, he places another garbage bag in the garbage, wearing sunglasses. At 17:14, he leaves the building with the same black t-shirt on carrying luggage and wearing sunglasses."

I never testified at my trial. I'm assuming people think because I pled guilty to these acts and presented an NCR defense I did the crime. In fact it is a common legal tactic to plead guilty even if you're not in order to present the best legal defense. I was never ever diagnosed as a psychopath, I've seen over 20 doctors and experts. They all agree I don't fit that criteria. Everything the media has falsely written makes for good fiction. I will say this. I had two residences in Montreal, one for work and a private residence. The apartment people see in the news was just for work. I only brought dates there. A lot of shady people resided there, and

I spoke to none of them. I'm told many of them made false claims, someone like me wouldn't talk to people like that. Complete lies.

I will say this about that night. People have physically forced me into situations threatening my family and myself. The people involved in my case were never sought out. The Montreal and Toronto Police are completely corrupt. These cops were too focused on notoriety and had tunnel vision on me. I was framed many times. Society is force fed media propaganda. It's phenomenal.

There was a victim of Luka Magnotta. His life was taken in the most horrific and humiliating way that one could imagine. He was not just murdered, he and his corpse were played with and abused, and then the act was placed on the Internet, for all to see.

Jun Lin was born Dec. 30, 1978, in China. He was from the industrial city of Wuhan where being gay is something people usually keep to themselves. Later he moved to Beijing, but it was widely known amongst his friends and family that his dream was to move to Canada. He eventually realized his goal and immigrated to Canada to study computer science at Concordia University located in Montreal, he worked at a convenience store to get by.

His family didn't know that he was gay. They were always wondering when he would meet a woman; when he would settle down and start a family. In fact Lin had settled down for a brief time. He met a boyfriend in Canada, whom he had been with for a year and a half. They had broken up just weeks before he met Luka Magnotta when he ostensibly replied to Luka's Craigslist add looking for sex with a side of bondage.

I have no doubt that Jun Lin was an interesting man. He has been described as a gentle person and also one who was brave. He was also complicated. Most of us are. It would be nice to give more attention to Jun Lin, but just as in all stories about Luka, he is always the star and he will be in this story as well.

While to many of us meeting someone in such a manner as through a Craigslist ad for sex is beyond bizarre, to others meeting in this manner is part of the fun. Anonymous, and sometimes dangerous. Sex with strangers isn't everyone's scene, but it goes on every day. To some people the thrill is the anonymity. There are websites around, if you know where to look, that will tell you where to go to find sex in your hometown. It might be the men's room at a department store at the mall, or it might be on some abandoned trail on the outskirts of your city, places where men have sex, get back in their cars, and go on their way back to their lives.

Recently Craigslist shut their "casual encounters" section of their website down, but not long ago it was the place to go if you wanted anything from a quick hookup in a bathroom stall, or a spanking, or maybe a little foot play, a threesome, or maybe even if you wanted to be tied up and tortured, just a little bit. What Lin did wasn't all that odd, not in the grand scheme of things, but he did have incredibly bad luck.

The ad that Lin answered was looking for someone to have a "threesome, party and play." According to Luka the third person in the threesome was Manny. Luka was to be the one tied up. Lin was to do whatever he wanted to Luka. Manny was going to be behind the camera. Doing his thing.

Lin met Luka at a McDonalds near a local Metro station. Apparently, they both were fine with what they saw, at least enough to continue the transaction, because they then walked back to Luka's place. Once they got there they smoked some weed. Although Luka said he only took one hit, one has to stay under control in these situations after all, they talked about having sex, what they were going to do, limits, and all that.

Lukas cellphone rang, he didn't pick it up. He knew it was Manny, but he was in the middle of something. He was working it, making sure everything went off okay. Lin wanted something to drink, all Luka had was wine, so he gave him some. Lin wanted Magnotta to drink too, but Luka said no, he didn't really like booze, it wasn't his thing, but Lin insisted, so he had a little just to make his guest happy.

At this point Magnotta told Lin his friend Manny wanted a threesome, was he up for it? What about that? Lin said no thank you. Not today, not in the mood. That would have been fine with Luka, but Manny kept calling and calling and calling. He wouldn't stop. The phone rang and rang. At one point Luka picked the phone up. Manny told him to turn on the webcam, so he could be a part of what was going on. He always wanted to be in control. So Luka did and Manny and Lin chatted for a bit. It seemed to go okay.

Why didn't he ignore Manny's calls? That question seems to make sense. But Luka couldn't.

Manny wouldn't take no for an answer. He never did. He pushed and pushed. He forced Luka to do all sorts of things.

Luka was going to leave the country soon anyway and be away from him. He couldn't wait. Manny knew people in the government that would mess with Luka. He knew bad people who would hurt him. Sometimes Manny punched Luka in the head. He had to do what Manny said.

At one point Luka had written his former lawyer Romeo Salta and told him forty-two things that Manny had done to him. Some of them were "Made me drink alcohol when I didn't want to," "Made me watch television shows I didn't want to then hit me when I changed the channel," "Told me if I went to see any doctors he would kill me, said he was always outside watching me," "Forced me to eat animal parts," and perhaps worst of all "Made me have sex with his puppy and numerous cats."

At some point during that night Luka's mind started to race. He felt weird. It would have been nice to be alone, to not have to deal with all of this, but Manny was on the webcam talking to Lin, telling him to tie up Magnotta. Turn the camera on. Keep the camera on. Manny wanted to see it.

Maybe Manny was going to put this on the web like he did with the cat videos. Luka hoped not.

After Luka was tied up, Lin started fucking him really hard. Riding him. It hurt. Luka wanted it to stop and said so, but Manny said to keep going. Lin did. It seems like everyone does what Manny tells them to do.

Luka started yelling for Lin to stop. It hurt so much. He begged Lin to stop. He needed this to end. He felt stupid. Used. Pathetic. Lin finally stopped and untied him and then Luka went in the bathroom and cried. When he came out he was going to ask Lin to leave but Manny kept calling and calling and calling, over and over again. When Luka finally answered Manny said, "Why the fuck don't you answer the phone, I called you like twenty times!"

There were some other voices too talking to Luka, most of the time he couldn't hear what they were saying. Luka told Manny he wasn't feeling well and Manny said, "How do you know it is not something he put in your drink? How do you know he is not working for the government? He could be an agent." Manny told him to look outside for cars with tinted windows, Luka did but he didn't see any, but he did see a black car. He knew what that meant.

He was scared. He was dizzy. He heard voices saying, "Kill him; he is an agent." Luka's mind started racing. He blacked out. He felt something wet. He heard voices. They said, "Cut it." He felt sick. He threw up.

Manny said, "I'll handle everything."

Luka was shaking all over. Manny told him to start throwing things away in the trash. Lin was on the bed with no arms and no legs.

Manny said, "Put the body in the tub." Manny again told Luka to throw things away. He didn't remember much after that. It was like someone was inside, taking him over. Like a spirit. Luka's body slowed down like someone was making him walk and talk as slow as can be, and then something would speed him up, back and forth, fast and slow.

A building superintendent called the Montreal Police on the twenty-ninth.

It seemed that he had found what might be the remains of a human body in a suitcase left outside of an apartment building. The suitcase smelled bad, and flies were all around it. It was left next to a pile of discarded furniture and other pieces of random garbage that were scattered about. The building superintendent opened the bag and looked inside. What he saw was enough to make him call the police. When they arrived the police confirmed that what was inside was a human torso, in other words a body missing limbs and a head. The suitcase had been there for several days.

Later on that day the Conservative Party headquarters in Ottawa received a package containing a human foot. Shortly afterwards a package containing a hand was intercepted intended for the Liberal Party of Canada in Ottawa. One doesn't have to be the best detective in the world to figure out the torso in the suitcase, and these events might have something in common. The police began investigating. A camera at a post office not far from the apartment where the body was found captured the image of a man who looked quite the same as a man shown on video carrying bags of trash outside of the apartment building where the body was found. It was soon figured out that the suspect was Luka Rocco Magnotta, resident of Apartment 208.

When the police entered his apartment, they said it smelled like chemicals and "death." They found some blood on a table. They found bills with Luka's name on them. They found a receipt for a pizza.

Close to this same time, the police became aware of a video that was circulating around the Internet. It looked like it was of a killing and dismemberment, and it had become rather obvious that the police were dealing with very much the same thing, but the video couldn't be real. I mean, could it? The video was found on a website called Kevin.666 and was called *Time to Shake Things Up a Bit.*

It then started to appear other places, including the shock website Bestgore.com under the name of *1 Lunatic, 1 Ice pick.* BestGore.com is a rather interesting site, filled with categories, such as *Impalement, Hanging, Burn Victim*, and *Beheading.*

Its owner is a man named Mark Marek who once told me in an interview that was in a book called *Subversive* "The content published on Best Gore is nothing more and nothing less than a reflection of what really goes on in the world. Pretending that it doesn't go on by not reporting on it, will not mean that all that foulness does not take place. I've always been a strong proponent of freedom of the internet and the free flow of content and ideas on the information superhighway. The other part of the right to freedom of expression is the right to access to information. And so I established Best Gore so the information that is routinely censored by the mainstream press, is available to those who are interested. It is not forced on anyone, so all those who prefer to live with rose colors shades on can just ignore the site. But those who do want to see reality, ought to have access to content that exposes it. After all, real life is uncensored."

Mark puts a lot of pretty messed up things on his site, but he never ended up being prosecuted for it before Luka's video. He got a six months conditional sentence for "Corrupting Morals."

The police found out that Magnotta had left the country on a flight for Paris. He purchased the ticket under his own name on the website lastminute.com. He bought the ticket when he was at the airport and bought a return ticket for June 1.

Luka told me of this: *Another huge lie is that I was on the run. I was never on the run ever from anyone. I had no idea anyone was ever looking for me. I used all my own credit cards and passport. I was relocating to Germany and a pedophile predator befriended me and begged me to* *allow him to help me. He took me to nightclubs and had sex parties. I was not into him at all, so one morning I simply told him goodbye and that I didn't want to be his friend. He was also a thief who stole $16,000 in cash from me and another $5,000 from my credit and debit cards. He continued to express his love, and I continued to reject him, I walked to the Internet café to meet a friend. I was watching an Ava Gardner film, not researching myself which was widely and falsely reported. I also never proclaimed to the police 'you got me.'"*

I was completely relaxed and looking forward to my new home in my new country. I had not a care in the world and enjoyed going out at night. Since I rarely used the Internet I had no idea anyone was searching for me.

According to the Watts report, the human torso found in the grey suitcase outside was identified as belonging to a man. It had lacerations and penetrating wounds to the abdomen and the genitalia were intact. The police began investigating all of the garbage at the scene and discovered several garbage bags containing items possibly related to the crime. This included several items of clothing, some of which were stained with what looked like blood. It also included: latex gloves, cleaning products, a camera, a cellphone, a blue marker, a laptop, and a coat. Other bags contained a screwdriver, a hammer, a vinyl tablecloth covered in blood, an electric "Mastercraft Multi-Crafter" saw, a dead black and white puppy, a leg and two arms with the hands cut off, a Casablanca poster, and a left leg without the foot. In the apartment, the mattress was found to be soaked in blood. It was wrapped in plastic with duct tape. A forensic assessment using luminol indicated that the apartment was tainted with blood, particularly in the

living room between the bed and the sofa. Blood was found on the floor in the kitchen and in the bathroom as well as many bloodstains in the hallway in the apartment."

A message reading, "If you don't like the reflection don't look in the mirror, I don't care" was written on a wall.

Police found a camera and memory cards at the crime scene, which is really kind of amazing when one thinks of it. One does all this and then throws everything in the apartment away and just leaves the camera?

The police felt what was found on the camera was the original material for the film circulating around the Internet. There were many scenes that didn't quite make the cut, such as when Luka lay on the bed and rubbed his genitals with Lin's dismembered right arm.

One could see it was Luka who did this. One could see his face.

Later a right hand and right foot was mailed to schools in the Vancouver area. The hand was mailed to False Creek School and the return address given was "L. Valentini" from St. Catharines, Ontario. Karla Homolka's sister had changed her name to Logan Valentini.

A note was in the package with the hand. It said "Roses are red. Violets are blue. The police will need dental records to identify you. Bitch."

8

The apartment people see in the news was just for work.
I only brought dates there. A lot of shady people resided
there, and I spoke to none of them. I will say this about
that night. People have physically forced me into situations
threatening my family and myself—Luka Magnotta

The following is, to the best of my knowledge, an account
of what transpired between May 24, 2012, the night Jun
Lin was last seen alive entering my son Luka's apartment,
through to June 4, when Luka was finally apprehended in
Berlin, Germany, and up to his extradition back to Canada
on June 18.

On Thursday, May 24, 2012, at approximately 10:00
p.m., a surveillance camera records Jun Lin and my son
Luka entering Luka's apartment building at 5720 DeCarie
Boulevard in the Snowdon District of Montreal. The camera
captures them a few minutes later approaching the door of
Luka's second-floor apartment. Around midnight the same
night, Jun Lin sent his former boyfriend a text message.
Investigators revealed that the murder of Jun Lin took place
sometime between midnight and 2:00 a.m.

At approximately 2:00 a.m., my son Luka is seen on the
video surveillance camera leaving his apartment building
wearing what is thought to be Jun Lin's yellow T-shirt,
which the young man appeared to be wearing when they
arrived. Surveillance video also captured Luka placing
several garbage bags into a waste container in the basement
garbage area of his building. Over the course of that day,

May 25, and the next day, May 26, my son's steps are caught on several surveillance cameras.

His activities over those two days included the acquisition of a suitcase that was later found to contain Lin's torso. He is also seen at two post offices. He booked a round-trip plane ticket to Paris, France. He also made a number of phone calls to the 705 region in Ontario. My mother, Melissa, my father, and I all lived in that region. Later in the investigation, the police

and forensic psychologists questioned us about a brief call that Luka made to a cellphone my mother and Melissa were sharing at the time. Neither of them recalled receiving a call from Luka. I had emailed Luka around May 25 or 26 just to say hi and to tell him I loved him, as I usually did. I can't remember if he called back or emailed me, but I do recall that he did respond, saying something like "You caught me just in time, I'm shutting down my email and leaving for California soon to start my new life."

You never imagine that a simple message or phone call to your son will later become a piece of information in a crucial timeline surrounding a murder investigation. At the time, it seemed so insignificant, but later that message haunted me. I remember racking my brain to try to recall every little detail, but I kept coming to the same conclusion: there was nothing out of the ordinary or suspicious about it at all. Luka had already told me about his plans to move to California, and he had closed down his email accounts before. This was not unusual behavior for Luka.

On Saturday, May 26, an eleven minute video titled *1 Lunatic, 1 Icepick* surfaced on the Internet, on a website called Bestgore.com. A U.S. lawyer by the name of Roger Renville came across the video and was concerned. The video appeared to depict a real murder taking place.

That same day, my son was seen arriving at Pierre Elliott Trudeau airport in Montreal. Luka purchased the plane ticket through the website lastminute.com at 20:59

on May 26, 2012, when he was already at the airport. He used his legal name "Luka Magnotta." The return ticket was for June 1, 2012. Police obtained a copy of Luka's passport and confirmed that he had left the country on May 26, 2012. He boarded Air Transat flight #613 bound for Paris, France. Luka is seen on camera carrying a satchel bag and wearing a Mickey Mouse T-shirt and a wig. Luka was the last passenger to board the flight. He took seat #33A, next to the window.

On Sunday, May 27, lawyer Roger Renville alerted Canadian and U.S. police about the murder video that had been posted online. He later stated that the police on both sides of the border were very skeptical about the video's authenticity.

That same day, Luka arrived at Paris's Charles de Gaulle Airport, and later that day checked in to the four-star Novotel hotel in central Paris.

Jean Christophe Robert, a nudist who Luka got to know on a dating website, received a text message from Luka that day. In it, Luka told him that he had arrived in Paris, and that he wanted to meet Jean at his apartment in the northwest part of the city. Jean gave Luka directions to his apartment, and Luka apparently spent the night there.

The next day, Luka purchased a new cellphone registered to Novotel and checked into the two-star hotel La-Soummam. He made his reservation to stay there until June 4, using identification in the name of Kirk Trammell.

On Tuesday, May 29, back in Canada, police were called when a suspicious blood-stained package arrived and was partially opened at the Conservative Party headquarters in Ottawa. Later that afternoon it was confirmed that the package contained a human foot. Police responded again when a second package was intercepted by Canada Post employees at the Ottawa postal terminal. Before that package was opened, it was x-rayed by police. They discovered it contained a human hand. This package was addressed to the Liberal Party headquarters.

In Montreal's Snowdon District, a suitcase was discovered containing a human torso near a garbage bin at 5720 DeCarie Boulevard. When police combed through the crime scene, they discovered paperwork identifying a suspect. At 11:30 p.m., police search Apartment 208 — my son Luka's apartment. Though they had not released any information to the public yet about who the resident of that apartment was, the Montreal police notified the Peterborough police and asked them to come to my home and to my mother's and Melissa's home to investigate if Luka was at either residence and to inquire if we had any information about his whereabouts. The same day, friends reported Jun Lin missing to the Consulate General of the People's Republic of China in Montreal.

On Wednesday, May 30, the police confirmed that both packages containing body parts had originated in Montreal. This was when I got that horrible feeling that Luka was involved. That afternoon a press conference was held, during which the Montreal police named the murder suspect. It was then I learned that my son, Luka Rocco Magnotta, was the prime suspect in the crime and that a Canada-wide warrant was being issued for his arrest.

My world collapsed that day right before my eyes.

Late Wednesday night, the media reported that a letter had been attached to the severed foot in the first package discovered. The note stated, "Four more body parts have been mailed out. Police and postal officials are working to track down those packages."

The next day, May 31, Interpol issued a "Red Notice" to its 190 member-countries (under common law this is considered a "provisional request from Canada for his extradition"). The international manhunt for my son had begun. Luka was last reportedly seen by La-Soummam hotel staff in Paris. Later it is revealed that he boarded a bus that day and travelled from Paris to Berlin.

On Friday, June 1, Montreal police identified the torso victim as 33-year-old Jun Lin, a Chinese computer student who had been studying at Concordia University and had been reported missing a couple of days earlier.

On June 2, the Montreal police announced that they would be laying additional charges against Luka. The following day, authorities confirmed that Luka was spotted in France but warned that he could still be on the move.

On Monday, June 4, 2012, at 2:00 p.m. local time, my son was arrested without incident in a small internet café in Berlin, Germany. The café was located near the center of the city. When the café owner recognized Luka, he went out onto the street to flag down police. He hailed down a van carrying seven young officers from a police training school. When the officers entered the café on Karl Marx Strasse and approached my son, they asked him his name. Luka rambled off some fake names then told them who he was. He was taken into custody.

The Montreal police notified me that my son had been arrested without incident. I was so relieved that he had been found and that he was unharmed.

Luka was taken to Berlin's Moabit Prison where he was held in a small cell. The following day he would go before a judge. When Luka made his brief court appearance at a massive police station, he stated that he would not fight the extradition to Canada.

Back in Canada, on Tuesday, June 5, two schools in Vancouver received packages containing Jun Lin's other hand and foot. And three weeks later, on July 1, a tip led police to a Montreal park, where they discovered Jun Lin's skull.

Dr. Barth, a forensic psychiatrist, began seeing my son daily after Luka was transferred to another holding facility in Berlin. Luka was considered a VIP patient at Dr. Barth's facility because of the seriousness of his alleged crimes, his status as a foreigner, and the media scrutiny surrounding the case. The doctor expected to have Luka under his care for a longer period of time, but the extradition process moved very quickly. By the time Dr. Barth's short-term assessment of Luka was completed on June 18, Luka was being prepared for his extradition.

When Luka's extradition day arrived, and I found out how he was going to be transported home, I couldn't believe it. I was shocked, dumbfounded actually. This can't be true, I thought. I learned that Luka would be flown home from Germany aboard one of the Canadian military's CC-150 Polaris Airbus transport planes. The police claimed that no commercial flight would accept him and that he needed to be transported on a direct flight. The reason given for this was that, in the event of an international layover, Luka could have tried to claim asylum in another country.

The military aircraft Luka was to be brought back on could be configured to accommodate prominent passengers such as the prime minister, foreign dignitaries, the governor general, and even members of the royal family. Along with the flight crew, six armed officers, including at least one that would be armed with an assault weapon, and Canadian forensic psychiatrist Dr. Joel Watts would be escorting my son back to Canada. Federal sources also said that the plane would be carrying German and Canadian officials, RCMP officers, and Canada Border and Security Services agency personnel. Dr. Joel Watts sat next to Luka, who was handcuffed and shackled during the flight.

The direct flight from Germany to Canada took approximately twelve hours. It was a very controlled extradition operation. There was, of course, huge media and public attention surrounding this very high-profile case. In my opinion the authorities amped up the attention when the decision was made to transport Luka back by military plane. This was the first time in Canadian history that an extradition had been handled this way. Many public taxpayers became outraged at the huge expense of the entire operation. The flight from a Cold Lake military base to Germany and back to Canada cost an estimated rate of $15,505 per hour. The round trip took nearly twenty-four hours. That's a total of $370,570!

To break it down, maintenance, hangar fees, crew salaries, and fuel: $6,420 per hour. Hotel estimate for eight crew members to stay overnight in Berlin, Germany: $1,300. Catering, $3,500 total ($2,000 of that in Germany's capital and $1,500 in Montreal). These figures were contained within documents obtained under the Access to Information Act.

This tally does not include costs assumed by other Canadian police forces involved in my son's extradition. The way this extradition was handled was ludicrous. The Canadian government and the prosecution capitalized big time on this. I believe that because this case was drawing so much media and public attention from around the world the Canadian government decided to go big on the extradition operation. They did this to hype up the media and piss off the public and make my son appear more dangerous than he actually was. In my opinion many law enforcement agencies and officials pushed for these drastic measures to exploit the hell out of the situation and make it impossible for my son to receive a fair trial.

9

I felt just fine actually. I was completely relaxed and looking forward to my new home, my new country. I had not a care in the world. Since I rarely used the Internet, I had no idea anyone was searching for me—Luka Magnotta

While Luka was who knows where, I remained in hiding, a prisoner in my own home. I found it almost impossible to leave the house. I was scared of being ambushed by the media. I was terrified that someone would seek revenge on me or my family for what Luka had done and try to kill or hurt us.

My daughter Melissa received a phone call one day from a man claiming to be a U.S. Marshal working for Interpol. She was very skeptical; we didn't trust anyone. We were always on the lookout for media snoops, people who were angry with us, Luka's crazy followers, and curiosity-seekers. We were becoming paranoid. But when Melissa contacted the Peterborough Police to investigate, they verified the man's credentials, so Melissa phoned him back.

The marshal was pretty impressed that she had checked him out before agreeing to speak with him. He was seeking Melissa's help with tracking Luka down. Luka had emailed Melissa, while the manhunt for Luka was underway, using an email account and name she was familiar with. The email read, "How does it feel to be the sister of a murderer?"

The Peterborough Police provided my daughter with a high-tech laptop to use in order to assist the U.S. Marshal. The authorities didn't want anyone to know that Melissa was working with them, so every measure was taken to keep it under wraps. A Peterborough Police officer dressed in a college hoodie and jeans came to her house that night after dark to drop off the laptop. Melissa then got on the phone with the US Marshal and they began their intense night-long task of searching the web to find clues, so they could track down Luka. They worked tirelessly through the night trying to sort through the abundance of online information that my son Luka had allegedly put there. My online accounts were searched through, as well. I was never able to access those accounts again or recover any of the information contained within them.

As the situation with Luka unfolded, we all still had matters that we needed to deal with, places to be, and business to take care of — life keeps on moving, even in a crisis. My kids had taken a few days off school, but soon it was time for them to go back. Of course, there was talk all over the schools about their brother Luka Magnotta. Cruel comments were being made and lots and lots of questions were being asked. It was a nightmare for them, one that neither they, nor anyone else could never have imagined.

The days of the manhunt were beginning to feel like years. The kids were having a very difficult time dealing with the situation. The media continued to harass them daily as they travelled to and from school. Numerous cruel things were being said to them and rumors were circulating through both of their schools like wildfire. I was furious. Police officers, social workers, teachers, and guidance counsellors were called upon by me to help my children.

I was having a complete meltdown by this point. I even considered asking the police if it would be a good idea for me to make a public plea to Luka urging him to turn himself in. My thoughts were everywhere and nowhere. A wave of panic came over me. My son had been missing for days, I thought. What if he was dead?

It's a devastating feeling not to know where your child is. Although he was being described throughout the world as a vicious killer and a dangerous fugitive, he was still my son. I was being flooded with questions from family and friends: Where do you think he is? Why do you think he did it? Has he contacted you? It just seemed to go on and on. And I didn't have any of the answers; I knew as much as everyone else did.

Luka and Anna

I also missed my parents; I hadn't seen them in days. They were afraid to come to my house, and I was afraid to leave it. I felt like a prisoner. Then came the phone call on June 4, 2012. It was the Montreal Police. In a thick French accent, the officer on the other end of the line informed me that my son was in custody and that he had been arrested without incident in an internet café in Berlin. We talked briefly, and he let me know that he would be meeting with the Lin family soon. I asked him to please pass on a message to them from our family. I wanted them to know the deep sorrow, sympathy, and pain we were feeling, and that words could never express how devastated and heartbroken, we felt and would always feel. The officer said he would pass on our message, and then he offered his condolences to our family as well. He said he hoped that one day we would find closure.

Soon, the stories of the arrest were front-page news, and the media was back and revved up again. It was a relief for me to know that Luka was fine, but our nightmare was far from over.

I clearly remember the extradition day. I was at home, still in hiding from the world, and decided to watch the media coverage of my son's arrival back to Canada. It was such a difficult thing. It was impossible to ignore but to watch the news brought me intense anxiety and pain.

There in front of me on the TV screen I saw a large military plane. Suddenly, my son was being escorted down the stairs by law enforcement next to Joel Watts, the psychiatrist. Luka was wearing a green, long-sleeved shirt and jeans. He was hand-cuffed in the front. My mind just could not comprehend what I was seeing. This was my boy. My child. I kept thinking is this real, is this really happening? At that moment, I felt that what was happening to me, to my family, was the worst thing in the world. It had suddenly become very apparent to me that this horrendous situation was going to be more difficult and more extensive than I could ever have imagined.

I continued to watch the coverage in a state of utter shock. My son was escorted across the tarmac of Montreal's Mirabel Airport to a motorcade of police vehicles that waited with flashing lights. There were media cameras everywhere.

I watched paralyzed as my son stepped into an unmarked van that would take him away to be interrogated for murder.

There would never be enough tears to express the deep sorrow I was feeling at that moment. I began to cry uncontrollably. I cried for my son; I cried for Jun Lin and his family; I cried for my family, and I cried for myself.

There was so much more to come, things I never thought I would have to deal with or be involved in. I overthought everything until my brain was raw. I realized that nothing was ever going to be the same or normal again. My entire view of the world was quickly becoming way out of focus. The situation was making even the simplest everyday things so much more difficult. Friends and neighbors were bringing me groceries and food because I couldn't go out shopping; mail had to be brought straight up to the front door, then they just decided to hold it at the post office; windows, doors, blinds, and curtains had to stay closed twenty-four seven. I felt ill from not having fresh air and sunshine. I even had to hide under a makeshift tarp fort on the back porch if I wanted to have a smoke outside, and believe me, at this point I needed my smokes more than ever. Reporters were hiding everywhere, even in the trees. I was emotionally spent and found myself growing increasingly depressed. I reached out for help from a local crisis center and sought medical attention. I received counselling and was prescribed medication to help me cope.

To say that we all were having a hard time mentally is an understatement. Melissa, my mother, and I talked a lot, and we came to the conclusion that the only way Luka could ever have done something this horrific was if "evil" had taken him over. We soon became convinced this was what had happened, and we all decided to remove any and all reminders of Luka from our homes. Out of sight, out of mind, I guess. It felt to us as if Luka was dead; "evil" had taken over him, and he was gone. My mother went through her house and gathered every single photo she had of Luka and ripped them to shreds. Then she threw out everything he had ever given to her. Melissa threw out everything but a white shelf and a balloon lamp that Eric had given to her when they were little kids. She packed up the photos, put them in her car, and then drove over to my place. We took all his photos down from the walls and went through every photo album, taking out every picture of him or with him in it. Then we went through the house and gathered up everything that he had given me over the years. I asked Melissa to put all the photos she had brought with her in the box with mine. Though I completely agreed at the time with getting everything linked with Luka out of sight, I couldn't bring myself to destroy the photos of my son or the special keepsakes he had given me. Into the photo box, I put all the newspaper articles about Luka and all the media correspondence letters I had received and taped it shut. I marked it "Photos" and drew a large sad face beside it. Melissa said we needed to move the stuff out of the house and into storage somewhere if I intended to keep it. But I didn't; I put it all away in a spare room, and there it stayed, unopened until Luka requested some of the photos while he was in Rivière des Prairies Institution awaiting trial.

10

I never posted the video online. That's a lie. How can anyone prove who posted a video on line unless you see them do it? Ill-informed armchair detectives assume it was me—Luka Magnotta

Around mid-June 2012, I received a phone call from one of the local police officers. He informed me that the Montreal Police were sending two investigators from the serious crimes unit to interview me, my mother, and Melissa, and they would also like to interview any other family members who were willing to speak to them. The two law enforcement agencies facilitated a date, time, and a place for the meeting. For safety and privacy reasons, they felt it would be best for us all to meet at the Peterborough police station.

We had a family meeting to discuss it. My mother refused to attend, telling us it would kill her to be put through that. My father also declined, as did my son Conrad, who had just moved to Mississauga with my cousin Tim to get away from the chaos in Peterborough and seek employment. We didn't put the request out to extended family members, just those in the immediate family. I really wanted my brother Eldon to come with Melissa and me, and he agreed and said he wanted to be there for me.

When the day came and we headed to the police station, both Melissa and I were very nervous and upset. We didn't know what to expect. When we got there, however, we were told that the Montreal investigators had just informed them that they would have to postpone our meeting for a day or two and apologized for the delay. They had gone to Toronto first to conduct some other business pertaining to the investigation, and it was taking longer than anticipated. A day or two later we set out to go down to the police station again. It was very hot that morning, and I sat quietly in the car and looked out the window thinking I don't want to do this, that was the very last thing I wanted to do in the entire world. When I looked over at Melissa, she was just sitting there quietly, too, and I knew what she was thinking and feeling by the sad look in her eyes. She looked devastated. I didn't want my poor little girl to have to go through any of this, either, and I started to cry.

Melissa and I held hands as we walked up to the front doors of the police station; Eldon walked beside us. Once inside, we were greeted by one of the local officers, who escorted us to a conference room to wait for the Montreal investigators. My anxiety was through the roof by this point, so I took one of my prescribed sedatives to calm my nerves. Apprehension and tension filled the room as we waited. We had tried to prepare ourselves for this day, but it was impossible, and now it was staring us in the face.

When the investigators came in, they introduced themselves, sat down, and spoke to the three of us as a group first. They explained that they were from the Serious Crime Unit in Montreal and that they were there to question us as well as to answer any questions we might have for them. It was a surreal feeling sitting in front of the police about to be questioned in a murder investigation involving my son. My mind was racing, my mouth was dry, my heart was pounding, and I felt ill and weak. They explained to us that we would be taken one at a time into a private room and questioned individually. After that, they would speak to us again all together.

Melissa was taken in first, and she was gone for approximately an hour and a half. The interrogation questions included the following: they wanted to know what relation certain people were to Luka; what her and Luka's relationship was like; she was asked several questions regarding a certain apartment Luka had once rented in Toronto where he had painted the walls red; when and why did he change his name? When did she last hear from him? See him? Who was the child with him in the photos he had put online? He had been claiming that the child was his son, but it actually was one of his nephews.

I was taken in next. The two detectives escorted me to another room. They motioned to me to take a seat, then both of them sat down across from me at the table. They advised me that they would be recording the interview. The detectives explained that they were there to gather information to help piece together this puzzle, to try and figure out not just what happened, but why.

I felt disconnected from reality. I remember telling the detectives I was on medication, and I asked them for some water. My mouth was so dry that I was having difficulty speaking. My recollection of the precise questions they asked me, and my answers and statements are vague. I remember being asked if I had any prior knowledge that Luka was going to commit this crime. This question was reworded a few times. I said at one point, "Do you think I knew? I didn't!" One of the detectives replied, "No, if we had reason to believe you did, this interview would be very different. We would have you in another room with a video camera rolling." I was asked if Luka was violent, what his character was like, if he had mental health issues, and about the last time I saw or spoke to him. I was asked about his life, his background, and about the trips we had taken together to Montreal and the Bahamas a few years prior. They wanted to know if he had ever been to Hollywood as they at one point thought he might be linked to an unsolved murder there known as The Hollywood Sign Murder. They inquired about what our relationship was like and why I thought he would do this.

At one point I lost it. I told them my son was dead, that evil had taken over him I started spewing incoherent answers, statements, and opinions. I was confused. My brain was in overload and went into shutdown mode. I wanted to be anywhere but in that room. They had been interrogating me for a couple of hours by this point. We took a break, and they escorted me back to the conference room. They then spoke with Eldon.

Eldon never shared much of his interrogation session with me. He said they wanted to know some background information and about what kind of person Luka was. While Eldon was being questioned, Melissa and I asked to go outside to have a smoke.

We lit our smokes and stood there shivering; even though it was a hot, sunny day. We just could not stop shaking. Melissa looked completely traumatized. We were so distraught that we could barely speak to one another. I remember Melissa saying, "Mama, this is bad, really bad. What are we going to do?" I kept saying, "I know, I know, I know." I felt the same way, but I didn't have an answer; all I could do was hug her. We locked arms and headed back inside.

When Eldon was brought back, I was taken in again. I don't remember much about the second session except being asked by the investigators if I had any questions for them. I said something along the lines of, "I don't want to know any more." I also remember them telling me that they really needed to speak to my mother and that they wanted her to come in and talk to them. She had made it very clear to us that she didn't want to talk to them; she wanted no part of this. They asked me to call her and impress upon her how important it was that they to speak with her. I called and told her what they said, but she still refused. When I relayed her answer to the investigators, they asked me to call her back and tell her they were willing to come to her house to speak with her when we were finished there that day.

She was still resistant to the idea, and I kept telling the investigators, "She doesn't want to do this; she said it would kill her." But they persisted. Melissa and I had hoped they would leave my mother out of this if we cooperated and came in to talk to them. My mother was hysterical on the phone, but finally reluctantly agreed to let them come and talk to her. I felt vile that my mother was put in this position. I knew what she was in for because Melissa and I had just experienced it. When they finished up with me for the second time, Melissa was taken in again. Eldon and I waited. It was evening now, and we'd now been there for several hours. When they brought Melissa back into the room, the investigators joined us, and we talked again as a group. We were thanked for our cooperation and told that they might be in touch with us again. I'm not sure what else was said other than that they wanted to follow us to my mother's house because they weren't sure of the way around town.

Luka in prison

We all left the police station, got in our cars and headed to my mother's place. I phoned her and told her we were on our way. She was very upset. She said she didn't want them to stay long; she just wanted to get it over and done with. We arrived at her house, and I brought them in. They introduced themselves and thanked my mother for agreeing to speak with them. They sat down with her at her kitchen table, set up their recording equipment, and began questioning her. She was basically questioned along the same lines as we had been. She was asked about a brief phone call that Luka had made to her number the day of or the day after the murder. She didn't recall talking to him. She was very uncomfortable, and she looked physically ill; her face was flushed, and she was emotionally drained. I can't remember what else was discussed. They didn't stay too long — maybe they realized the toll that this was taking on my mother. They thanked us again, packed up their notes and recording devices, and I walked them out.

After that experience I felt like I was losing my mind. I thought that I was before, but it was nothing compared to this. It made what was happening very real, and I couldn't cope with that. I had only heard about murder investigations. I never expected to be involved in one, and this was only the beginning. And it wasn't just "a murder" if there is such a thing. It was the possibly the most famous murder that Canada had ever seen, and almost certainly one of its most gruesome. As this investigation continued to unfold there was no avoiding the inevitable process that was to follow.

I wasn't in the right frame of mind nor did I have the physical strength to go see my son Luka at this point. It was June 2012. Luka was back in Canada, I believe he was processed at Regional Reception in Montreal first then placed at Rivière des Prairies Institution until his trial. None of the family went to see him. It was too much. We started having contact with him again in February 2013 before pretrial. I deeply regret that I wasn't strong enough from the beginning to be there for my son Luka in his time of need. Trial was not until September 2014. I was adamant from the beginning that I could not handle going to the trial, I just couldn't take anymore.

After Luka's arrival back in Canada, he was taken to the Rivière des Prairies detention center in Montreal. The next day, June 19, he appeared in court via a video link and pleaded not guilty to all charges. The five offenses he was charged with were

1. First Degree Murder

2. Committing an indignity to a body

3. Harassing Prime Minister Stephen Harper and other members of parliament

4. Mailing obscene and indecent material

5. Publishing obscene material

Two days later, Luka appeared in person at a high security Montreal courtroom and requested a trial by jury. That fall, on October 9, a pretrial conference was held between lawyers and the prosecution. There was much preparation to be done before the preliminary hearing was to be held the following spring.

Luka's team of lawyers were putting together a Not Criminally Responsible, or NCR, defense. Luka would have to go through extensive psychiatric assessments, family would be questioned by psychiatrists, and reports would be prepared for court. Luka's history including all his medical records would factor into the defense strategy.

On March 11, 2013, the preliminary hearing began. The evidence presented there was subject to a publication ban. Luka's defense team also requested that the media and the public be barred entirely from the hearing, but their request was denied the next day. A few days later, one of Luka's lawyers resigned, citing a possible conflict of interest.

During the hearing, the court heard from various expert witnesses, and video evidence was presented. Jun Lin's father attended the hearing. In the end, on April 12, 2013, Luka was indicted on all charges and a trial date was scheduled.

In these months that followed Luka's arrest, I existed in a somber fog. I was trying to process the gravity of this life-changing ordeal, but it was too much for me to handle. I moved twice. I was seeing my doctor weekly, as well as a clinical therapist. But I still felt lost. I didn't know how to cope and start living again. Nothing felt the same. One day blended into the next as the weeks and months passed by. I went through the motions, just existing, not really living.

Then one day Melissa told me she had been contacted by a woman who said she was a friend of Luka's. Luka had asked her to get in touch with us. Apparently, he wanted to talk to us. His friend who was a woman by the name of KC offered to set up a three-way call among us and Luka, who was still being held at Rivière des Prairies.

Melissa and I talked it over. A long time had passed, and his preliminary hearing was coming up soon. We both felt we were ready to talk to Luka again, we wanted to support him, but we were so nervous. We didn't know what to expect or what to say to him, but we figured he must really need us if he'd gone to these lengths to get in touch with us. We still loved him.

KC arranged a time for the call and informed us that it would be monitored, as all calls were at the prison. When the time came, Melissa and I sat side-by-side, holding hands, waiting for the phone to ring. When it did, Melissa answered and spoke to KC first. She then patched Luka through to us. Melissa spoke to him first. They asked how each other was and said they loved each other. I was in tears listening to my son and my daughter speak. Luka told Melissa that KC had been good to him, and that she was helping him get by. He wanted us to talk to her and encouraged us to get know her and trust her. When Melissa and Luka were finished talking she passed the phone to me. I pulled myself together as best I could and took the phone. When I heard Luka's voice my heart started pounding. I asked him if he was okay and told him I loved him. I asked him if he was receiving medical attention. I was worried as he sounded medicated and lethargic. He said he loved me and told me that yes, he was okay, and he was seeing doctors and working on getting well. I told him I was proud of him for that and very glad to hear he was taking steps to get healthy. That's what I'd always hoped and wanted for him.

He then asked if we could stay in touch, that he had missed us, could we write letters and talk on the phone. I didn't have to think about it. I said, "Of course." He also told me about KC, and how he wanted me to get to know her and to trust her; he told me she was helping him so much. I was skeptical, but I agreed to keep in touch with her because he asked me to, and it was obvious that she was a big part of his life now. The trust part was up in the air, though, and remained to be seen. Why was this woman in his life?

Over the next few weeks, Luka and I talked on the phone and wrote letters to each other. KC began trying to insert herself more and more into our family. She would talk to us when we called Luka, and then she started calling us directly. She knew an awful lot about us that she'd gotten both from Luka and from the extensive media coverage, but we knew next to nothing about her. Luka seemed to trust her completely, but we were still being very guarded, even though we were happy that he had a friend and were grateful that she'd been helping him out financially for a time.

We learned that KC lived in Montreal, was divorced, middle-aged, had four children, and worked at P.E.T. Airport. She told us she'd heard about Luka on the news around the time he was being extradited back to Canada from Berlin. She said there was word going around P.E.T Airport that the military plane with Luka may be landing there. She told us she felt drawn to him and was compelled to try to help him. She said she felt very sorry for him. Once he was placed at RDP, she started writing to him. He was leery about trusting anyone, but she convinced him that her intentions were good. Eventually, they started talking on the phone daily, and she began putting money into his canteen. She quickly became his confidante, and over the months they formed a very close friendship.

Luka told me he wanted me to come for a visit, so in March of 2013, I headed to Montreal. This would be the first time I'd see him since his incarceration. I was also going to finally meet KC, which I was less than excited about. She and I planned to meet in the parking lot of RDP prison. My boyfriend at the time accompanied me on the trip. He did all the driving, as I was on sedatives at the time and in no shape to drive. It was a very long road trip, I cried on and off most of the way there. I hadn't actually seen my son in person since the summer of 2010. I didn't know what to say to him without bringing up the current circumstances. How do you just talk to your son in this situation? I wondered what condition he would be in. I was very nervous and upset, as I knew it was going to be a very emotional, awkward, and stressful visit.

After seven long hours on the road, we finally pulled into the parking lot of RDP. We parked the car, but I stayed rooted to the seat. I couldn't move. I wasn't sure if I could actually go through with it. I stared at the big grey barbed-wire-fenced prison in front of me. I couldn't stop shaking. My boyfriend said quietly to me, "If you don't think you can do this, it's okay. We can just turn around and go home." I did my best to calm down and focus. I'd come a long way to see my son, and he was expecting me. I didn't want to let him down. No matter what he had been accused of doing, he was still my son, and I knew he needed me.

I took a few deep cleansing breaths, grabbed my purse, and got out of the car. I saw that KC was making her way over to me. She was a very flamboyant woman, nicely dressed, and she spoke with a French accent. She greeted me like she had known me forever. She had a bag full of stuff with her that she said were gifts for Luka that she was going to give to me, so I could bring them to him. We chatted for a bit as we lined up to go into the prison. Once inside, she came with me to the reception desk. She introduced me to the guards while speaking French. She was very friendly and flirty with them. I passed them my photo ID and was instructed to walk through a security scanner archway and then to proceed out the door and across the courtyard to the next building. My boyfriend and KC assured me they would stay in the waiting room until I returned. As I walked across the courtyard, I was shaking, and tears were starting to brim up in my eyes. I was so out of my element. I was not familiar with this process whatsoever. At no point in my life did I ever think I would be visiting my son under these circumstances. I reached the other building, went inside, and approached a reception desk where I was asked to sign in.

One of the guards made a call, but the only word I could understand was "Magnotta." Then he instructed me to go through a door and down the hallway to the private visiting room where our visit would take place. I had the bag of stuff that KC gave me. I wasn't sure what I was supposed to do with it. I found the parlor number and went inside. It was a small concrete room with a chair, a piece of glass separating my side of the room from the other. There was an empty chair on the other side of the room and behind it, a heavy security door with a little window. A small wooden counter-type ledge was on both sides of the glass. I could hear noise and commotion coming from the hallway behind the heavy security door. I sat down and kept my coat on because I felt unusually cold. I waited, and waited, and waited for probably about twenty minutes. I was trembling and trying not to cry again. Then I heard the security door being unlocked. I looked up at the window and saw my son being let in.

His face lit up immediately. He looked so happy to see me. I was stunned at how different he looked. He was heavier than I'd ever seen him in his life. He sat down, and we said hello to each other, and he thanked me for coming to see him. I couldn't help it; I started crying. He said, "Please don't cry. I love you." I told him I loved him too. Once again, I composed myself and tried to stay strong.

Our visit was being monitored, so we couldn't talk about anything involving the offense as it was a matter before the courts, and there was a trial pending, not that I am sure we would have anyway. Anything we said could be used as evidence during the trial. There were so many things I wanted to ask him and talk about, but I couldn't. We chatted about my road trip that I had taken to see him, he asked about family members and how they were doing, and he talked about KC.

He appeared to be medicated, so I asked him about his health and what kind of medical care he was receiving. He said he was seeing psychiatrists and that he had put on seventy pounds since May from the medication he was taking. He said he felt physically unhealthy at that weight. He asked me to be honest with him; did I think he looked fat and ugly?

I answered him honestly. "No," I said. "You were always very thin, and you could use a few extra pounds, and I think you look very handsome, as always!" I told him I had the bag of gifts for him from KC, and he informed me that I was to take it to the exchange table on the way out. He was only allowed a certain amount of personal items, so there would be a bag of items he was exchanging for the new ones waiting for me to pick up at the desk. He asked me to please give the old bag to KC. I agreed and relayed her message that she loved him. The visit was just under an hour long, and it went by fast. Before I knew it, it was time for us to say our goodbyes. I could feel myself choking up again and about to cry. I told him I loved him very much, and I would talk to him on the phone soon, would keep writing to him, and I would come back soon to visit. We stood up and kissed each other through the glass, pressed our hands together on the glass, and said goodbye.

As I backed up, I started to cry again. He said, "Please don't cry, sweetie, please don't cry. I love you." I said "I can't help it, I love you, too." I blew him kisses as I walked out the door. I saw him sit down to wait for the guards to come back for him. I slumped down on the floor in the hallway and leaned against the wall. My eyes were burning from trying to hold back the tears. I didn't want to end the visit this way. I dried my eyes, stood up, and looked in the window. He was still sitting there waiting with his hands folded and his head down; he looked so sad. I couldn't leave him that way. I opened the door and went back in. He sat right back up and smiled. He looked very surprised. I said, "I'm okay, I'm good now, I was just overwhelmed." I put on the biggest smile I could and gave him the thumbs up and a wink. I told him I loved him again and backed up, smiling all the way out. He looked happy when I left him this time. When I got out into the hall I broke down again, but that was okay; at least he'd seen me smiling and happy before I left.

I walked back down the hallway and out into the reception area to exchange the items. The guards were very nice to me, and they explained the procedure for bringing in items and the exchanging process. They showed me an itemized list of the items he could have and the quantities. I had to sign a waiver saying I was aware of what I was dropping off, and I was responsible if anything illegal was found when the items were searched. I unpacked the items and put them up on the table for them to repack, label, and process. They gave me Luka's old items in a large brown paper bag. I took out a used pair of slippers and held them close to me for a minute, then put them back in the bag. I thanked them, said goodbye, and headed for the door. I walked across the courtyard to the main building. The bag seemed so heavy. I felt weak and drained from my experience and could barely see where I was going through the tears. The cold was stinging my face and eyes as I entered the main building. The guards asked me if I was okay. I said yes, just overwhelmed. They returned my identification and I thanked them. It meant a lot to me how friendly and nice to me they were. I made my way to the waiting room; my boyfriend and KC got up to greet me.

KC was overly excited to hear about my visit, even though she could see I was visibly distraught. She asked my boyfriend and me if we were going to go back to her place, so she could show us where she lived, and we could meet her two youngest kids. KC and Luka had planned this little get-together; Luka really wanted us to go, so we could get to know his new friend. My boyfriend and I felt very uneasy about going; him more so than I, but we agreed.

We followed KC to the house, it took about half an hour or so. She lived in a nice, quaint little neighborhood. Her place was the top unit of a town home. We followed her up the stairs and made small talk along the way. When we got to the top of the stairs, she unlocked the door and pushed it open, then she said, "Welcome home, this is your home, too." I was taken aback by her comment, I found it very odd. She was being overly friendly way too quickly. We had just met each other. We went inside, and she gave us a quick tour. Her place was clean and nicely decorated and furnished. There were scented candles burning throughout the house. She introduced her son and daughter to us. They were very polite and friendly. She asked if we would like a drink. Luka had told her I liked vodka, so she bought it for me. I really needed a drink by this point, so I accepted; my boyfriend declined.

We sat in the living room and chatted for a bit then KC asked me to come into her bedroom with her, so she could show me some of the drawings and letters Luka had sent her. She had made copies of them. Several were posted up on her wall, and she had more in her filing cabinet drawer. She told me she kept all the originals in a safe deposit box. Very strange, I thought as I sipped my drink. Why would she lock all the originals in a safe deposit box like they were priceless artwork? Then KC started to tell me how much she loved and adored Luka, she called him her angel, her prince! It was all so weird. She said she and Luka talked for hours on the phone even when she was at work, driving, and shopping. He came first always. and she would always be here for him, we were told. My first thought was, either she is totally nuts and some kind of crazed stalker/Luka follower or she really has genuine feelings for him and loves him very much. I was swaying towards the former though rather quickly!

We went back into the living room and chatted a bit more. She emphasized how much she would really love to get to know all of Luka's family, and she would be there for us too. She stressed, "If any of you ever need anything, let me know!" We thanked her for her hospitality and told her it was time for us to get back on the road, as we had a long ride home. KC thanked us so much for coming and hugged us as we were leaving. All I could think was what a bizarre visit that it was. It was definitely the first of its kind for me, but of course I didn't expect to be in any of these situations.

Over the following weeks and months I stayed in regular contact with Luka by phone and mail. It was nice to have him back in my life, even under these horrific circumstances. All the while KC was aggressively trying to insert herself into our family. Other family members were growing very suspicious of her and wanted nothing to do with her. Melissa and I were the only ones who had been associating with her in any way. She had tracked Conrad down and tried to form a friendship with him, but he wasn't interested — he felt the same way as everyone else.

In March 2013 Luka asked me to call and speak to his lawyer, a man named Luc LeClair. He said it was important. I called, and the lawyer requested a meeting with Melissa and me. He wanted us to come to Toronto, so he could speak to us in person, so we set up an appointment. We had no idea we were opening a door that would be almost impossible to close.

Melissa and I headed to Toronto to meet with him, but when we arrived at his office, he wasn't there. When we called him on his cellphone, he said he didn't think we were coming because we hadn't called back to confirm. What? I thought. We had told him we were coming, where did call back to confirm come from? He said he wasn't near his office and asked if we would we mind meeting him at a downtown coffee shop instead. Since we'd come all that way, we agreed.

When Melissa and I arrived at the café, we had no clue what this guy looked like. We ordered teas, found a table, and started looking around for someone who looked like a lawyer. No one appeared as if they were expecting clients. About ten minutes later a casually dressed older man walked in. He recognized us both right off the hop. He pulled up a chair and sat down at the tiny table with us. We made small talk for a few minutes before getting down to business. I noticed he seemed nervous; he kept scanning the room. "I don't want anyone to hear what we're talking about," he said, "so let's move in closer to one another and talk quietly."

We scooted our chairs in even closer to each other until we were literally touching shoulders. The three of us huddled together like this over this tiny table and began discussing Luka's case. His aim was for Luka to be found Not Criminally Responsible for the murder. He felt they had a good chance to achieve that outcome. He told us that there were a couple of forensic psychiatrists involved in the case and that they were talking to Luka. He wanted us to speak with them, too. They really needed our input. We were his family, and we knew him best. He stressed that the information we could provide to them would be very beneficial to their assessments. Melissa and I agreed.

At the end of that meeting Melissa and I asked him if he was planning to subpoena us. He said no. We made it very clear to him that none of us in the family wanted to be forced into court to testify. We had all been through more than we could handle already. We explained that my parents were elderly and in failing health; they couldn't attend the trial or testify — it would kill them. They just wanted to be left alone to live out their remaining years in peace. However, Melissa and I assured him that we were both still willing to completely cooperate with the psychiatrists in any way we could to help Luka. We just didn't want to testify in court.

This was all happening around the time of the preliminary hearing, in March of 2013. We got in touch with the two forensic psychiatrists who were called upon to assess Luka and compile a report for the court. Luka's lawyer really hoped that one or both of them would find Luka NCR for his actions at the time of the crime. Melissa and I answered all the questions the psychiatrists asked us, and we offered up anything we could recall that might be helpful to them.

The psychiatrists asked about Eric's childhood, his education, if he was ever abused, if he was ever violent, family dynamics, his medical history (even as far back as my pregnancy with him), why he had changed his name and if he exhibited any unusual behaviors. One forensic psychiatrist Dr. Joel Watts, focused on specific questioning. He asked about certain places where Luka had lived, timeframes for changes in Luka's mental health, his upbringing, Luka's hospitalizations, schizophrenia was discussed at one point. I was never completely convinced that Luka had schizophrenia. I told that to the psychiatrist. I think that diagnosis was just thrown into Luka's medical file somewhere along the way. He was never extensively assessed. I do believe he might have a personality disorder. "Manny" was also discussed. My mother reluctantly agreed to speak to one of the psychiatrists, as well. We were in regular contact with Luka at that time, and we reassured him that we had spoken to the doctors.

Dr. Watts began repeatedly calling us. We had already cooperated to the best of our ability, but he wouldn't give up. He would have my mother in tears. She begged him to leave us all alone. We all told him everything he wanted to know, but he wanted more. There was no more. Luka's lawyer was doing the same thing. It felt like they were expecting us to come up with the "magic" word or phrase that would be the answer to make all this make sense and give some reason to this act that Luka was accused of, but of course we couldn't, we were just as confused, perhaps more so, than anyone else. The defense had a tough case on their hands, and it was crunch time.

On one occasion I even conveyed my feelings to Luka's lawyer. We were talking on the phone, and I could hear the desperation in his voice. He wanted me to make an appearance in the courtroom to show support for Luka. I refused. It wouldn't make a difference to the outcome, and I would be putting myself through another nerve-wracking ordeal. I would be all over the media. I couldn't handle it. Except for moral support for my son and to show the court that a family member had appeared, I being there would not have helped or hindered the verdict. I would just be present. In retrospect I wish I had of been strong enough to be there for my son, even if it was just to sit there and morally support him. I will always regret that I wasn't able to be there for him.

Part of the reason I didn't go was that I feared for my safety. People hated Luka, and if they couldn't get at him they might try to hurt me. To say my mental health was fragile, and my sanity was hanging by a thread at that point would be an understatement.

I explained to Luka's lawyer that we were fed up with being put through the wringer. We just wanted to be left alone and to support Luka from the shadows. I told him, "At the end of the day, we have done all that we can. It's out of our hands now. It's in the hands of the justice system. We all have to come to terms with that, or it will destroy us!"

As all this was going on, I made three more trips to Montreal to visit Luka. I went in May, July, and October. On one of those trips, Luka's lawyer called me on the way. He wanted me to meet with the media and make a statement; he thought it would look very good for the case if Luka's mother spoke publicly. He basically wanted me to make an appeal on behalf of my son, in the hopes it would influence the public's opinion of him and persuade the judge for some leniency in his sentencing. I thought it was a terrible idea, and I refused. I felt that it wouldn't make a difference one way or another, that it would only add fuel to the fire and give the public something else to talk about, and that it even had the potential to put us in danger. My mind was made up.

The public hated Luka. The media was grabbing every shred of information they could get their hands on and publishing it. Some of the information was true, but they were also publishing a lot of rumors, lies, and speculations as well. If I had agreed to make a public statement especially in the shape I was in, they would have had a field day with it. They would have put their own spin on it. It wouldn't have accomplished anything productive for Luka's upcoming trial. The world would just have more to talk about and pick apart.

Luka and I spoke one day from the courthouse phone that he was permitted to use while waiting in a private room. He was scared; I could tell by the tone of his voice. He pleaded with me, "Call my lawyer; you have to talk to the doctors again. My life is in your hands!"

I couldn't believe he had said that to me. That was an enormous burden to place on my shoulders. The reality and seriousness of this ordeal was finally sinking in, and he was panicking! I tried to explain to him that there was absolutely nothing more I could say to the doctors; we'd said it all already. I asked him if he realized the toll this was taking on my health and my mother's health. We were all suffering as a result of all this. He became unreasonable at that point and said, "I'm taking a break from everyone, I can't deal with this anymore!"

I couldn't deal with anything anymore as well, and felt that a break was definitely in order and very much needed. I was feeling completely helpless and very frightened about what lay ahead for Luka. But Luka's life wasn't in my hands. If it had been a few years earlier, I feel that perhaps I could have saved him, but Luka's life was going to be in the hands of a judge and jury very soon. I tried to help Luka and get help for him before this crime happened, and he tried to get help for himself as well. I was frustrated that Luka didn't feel he needed my help then, that the doctors he had reached out to for help let him down, and that the police didn't take him seriously when he reported the abuse he was going through.

As a family, we collectively decided that enough was enough. We were done. We immediately severed all ties with the remaining members of the inner core — KC, the lawyer, and the doctors.

I composed and sent a text message to KC informing her that under no circumstances was she to ever contact me or anyone in my family ever again. We ignored any and all phone calls and messages from the lawyer and the doctor. We didn't answer any calls that came in from numbers we didn't know. It felt good taking back some control of our lives.

Due to the persistence of unwanted callers, we eventually all had to change our phone numbers. However, when we closed the eye of the storm, and all forms of communication with the inner core ceased, we, of course, found ourselves no longer in the loop. From that point on, our only source of information was through the media. We were now outsiders looking in, just like the rest of the world.

Our family tried hard to resume somewhat of a normal life during that time, but it was difficult. We were struggling with a whole new set of problems. A bunch of feelings and emotions had been stirred up during our recent contact with Luka and his inner circle, namely KC. Opinions and comments were being exchanged between family members and disagreements broke out several times. Tension among us all was very high at the time.

Eventually, things settled down somewhat. I aimlessly fumbled with the pieces of the badly broken life I was left with, but my life's compass remained irreparable; I had no sense of my future direction. I felt as if I was lost.

Up until this point, I had avoided reading or watching anything about Luka in the press or on the internet. But as the trial approached, something changed. I wanted — needed — to read and see everything that was out there about Luka. I sat down in front of my computer every day and started searching. I couldn't stop. The magnitude of information I was discovering was staggering. I became obsessed. I desperately wanted to read and view everything I could find, which was completely the opposite of how I had felt before. My brain disconnected with everything except the Internet, and for the next several weeks in online searches for any and all information I could find on Luka was my mission. I read article after article, I watched all the news footage and videos I could find, including the murder video, *1 Lunatic, 1 Icepick*. It was surreal. I was completely numb. I felt no emotion whatsoever.

My thirst to know everything was overpowering me. The things I was reading and seeing about my son and our family would have devastated me before, but at that point I really felt nothing, absolutely nothing. It felt good not to hurt or care anymore.

I continued with my obsession until I was satisfied that I knew everything there was to know about my son and the case. I was completely informed and prepared to follow the trial. I truly believe I had lost my mind by this point. In my fragile state, I formulated a "trial plan." I would follow the trial from an impartial, unbiased position, as if I were a juror. I would follow jury protocol to determine a verdict. I would be "Phantom Juror Number Thirteen." was in it until the end.

11

*When idiots who did not witness any of the events and
who were not even there give their opinions, who cares,
they are completely irrelevant—Luka Magnotta*

As the trial date drew closer, Luka's lawyer hired a private
investigator to come to Peterborough. His job was to serve
me, Melissa, and my mother with subpoenas to testify as
material witnesses for the defense. We hadn't seen this
coming, as we had trusted Luke LeClair when he assured
us that he would not subpoena us. The PI found my mother
first, as her address was known to them, and she was
ambushed and served as she stood in her driveway. She
cried and begged the investigator to take it back. Of course,
he couldn't.

One served, two to go.

He was then on the hunt for Melissa and me. Melissa was
in her yard hiding in the shed when he served my mother. He
knew Melissa and my mom lived at the same address, so all
he had to do was wait her out.

My mom tipped me off, and I went into high-alert
mode. He stalked both of us for a couple of days in a cat-
and-mouse game. He would knock on the door and leave
notes and business cards. He even went to Melissa's place of
employment, which totally embarrassed and upset her, but
he didn't catch her. When he came around her house again,
he convinced someone else who was there to accept the
letter from him: Melissa was considered officially served.

I avoided him like the plague. I opened my door one day to go out and there he was, quietly standing on the other side of the door. I screamed at him and slammed the door in his face before he could serve me. He even trapped my youngest daughter Leeanna in the foyer between the doors trying to get her to accept the subpoena, but she freaked out and yelled at him. When he finally moved and let her out, he followed in his car as she biked away. I was fuming mad.

Melissa got in touch with her lawyer to see what our options were and if we could get out of these subpoenas. She also informed him of the tactics the private investigator was using to get to us. He saw us right away and explained that it would be next to impossible to quash a subpoena, but he was willing to help us fight them in any way that he could.

He began sending emails to Luka's lawyer conveying our position that we did not want to testify and the many valid reasons we had for not wanting to. The private investigator eventually slipped my subpoena under my door after several unsuccessful attempts to give it to me. I was considered served. Emails were exchanged back and forth between the lawyers for several days. We were at a standstill.

Our first and foremost priority was my mother. She was in poor health with dangerously high blood pressure. We worked to get her cut loose first. I took her to the doctor to get a letter stating the condition of her health. Our lawyer forwarded it to Luka's lawyer, and the defense team decided to excuse my mother from testifying.

The defense team remained firm that Melissa and I would still be testifying, as ordered by the court. Emails and phone calls continued between the lawyers. Melissa's lawyer Christopher Spear, officially took me on as a client pro bono.

I did not want to testify at the trial. I was a complete nervous wreck at the time. I was terrified that I was going to be killed if I appeared in public at the Montreal court. I truly felt that I would die if I went to that trial, whether it be from a heart attack or that I would be targeted by someone because I am Luka Magnotta's mother. I believed there were people out there who would go to such extreme lengths to get even or punish Luka by hurting one of us.

For the record, I fully cooperated with the police during the investigation and with the forensic psychiatrists —one whose findings were used in Luka's defense, and one whose findings were never used in court — during Luka's pretrial assessment process. I answered all the questions asked of me, and I provided as much insight and information as I could to them. I kept in contact with Luka's lawyer, Luc LeClair, as well, and I provided him with any requested information. I made it very clear to Mr. LeClair and to psychiatrist Dr. Joel Watts right from the beginning that I did not want to appear in person at the court to testify during the trial, and I provided them with my valid reasons. I was completely forthcoming with all information, and I had absolutely no problem with that information being submitted in writing to the courts to be used in my absence during the trial.

Melissa and I both went to our doctors and got letters explaining our health concerns. These were sent to Mr. LeClair, but no dice; we were informed we still had to testify. Our lawyer was drawing on every resource he had to help us.

It was getting down to the wire when a desperate measure was taken by Melissa and executed by our lawyer in an attempt to free her from the obligation to testify. Surprisingly it worked. Melissa was considered a hostile witness, and they cut her loose. That left only me, and I was still determined that I was not testifying. So, I decided against my lawyer's advice, that I would not appear in court, regardless of the consequences. I would let the court issue a warrant for my arrest. If I was going to be forced to go and be dragged off to Montreal, I was going kicking and screaming, but I still wouldn't testify. I'd rather sit in jail. And I'd have the media all over it; they'd been dying for a scoop all along. I even considered going into hiding until the trial was over and trying to escape from police custody if I was arrested. I honestly felt that I wouldn't come back from Montreal alive. At the eleventh hour, I was determined to be a hostile witness and cut loose, as well.

With that huge pressure off my shoulders, I could turn my focus back to my trial plan.

I stayed up-to-date with all the media coverage. On September 16, 2014, jury selection began. When the jury selection process was completed, the trial was scheduled to begin on September 29.

Our next step was to put a safety plan in place before the trial started. We set up meetings with several community agencies and collaborated with them to cover every base we could think of to ensure our safety and well-being during the next inevitable phase of our circumstance. We had school officials, Children's Aid, Victim Services, and the YWCA all on board to help us. The children's schools were put on high alert as we and the police felt that there was a potential risk that someone might want to harm the children because of who they were. They were prepared to handle the media and keep them at bay. The children would be watched at all times and escorted out to our vehicles. Taxis would be provided for transportation, if necessary, and if need be, a children's aid worker would go into the schools and take the children somewhere safe if we weren't able to get near the school because of the media presence. Our homes were inspected and things were modified to minimize the risk of us being harmed and to deter the media from coming onto the property. "No Trespassing" signs were posted; window coverings were changed, any and all personal items such as photos, mail, anything with our personal information, was hidden from sight. We were all given emergency cellphones to carry on us and to hide in our homes to use if we encountered a threatening situation. We were also instructed on how to handle ourselves if a threatening situation arose.

We even had a medical emergency plan. In the event that one of us had a medical emergency and needed to get to the hospital, we would not enter the hospital through the public door; we would have to use a secluded private entrance. Once inside the hospital, we would not be put in any public area or waiting room in case the media showed up. Preventative measures were taken for every possible scenario we, or the police, could think of. We were still on edge after all this planning, but we did everything we could to prepare ourselves for what was coming.

September 28, the day before the trial started, was my father's eighty-second birthday. I could not fall asleep. I just lay there thinking. "Today is my father's birthday and tomorrow my son stands trial for first-degree murder." I wondered what Luka was thinking, and I hoped he knew I was thinking of him and knew that I loved him. I reminisced for a bit about better days gone by, then I went over and over all of the information in my head that I had recently researched on the Internet. I thought about my family and the Lin family, I thought about the jurors, the media, the crazies … my mind was reeling.

Then, as if a door had slammed shut in my brain, all of a sudden, I felt calm. I closed my eyes and began to think about my obligations as "Phantom Juror Number Thirteen" that would begin the next day.

On September 29, 2014, the trial began. I got up early and went straight to my computer and started watching the media coverage from the Montreal courthouse. I stayed focused on my trial plan. I needed to find a way to follow the events unfolding in the courtroom. I learned that a few journalists would be present, so I found one who was going to live-tweet the proceedings, so I had a way to follow the trial as it was happening.

For the next several weeks, I stayed glued to my computer, following the trial via live newsfeed. I carefully read the testimony of every single witness and all the defense's and Crown's questions, cross-examinations, and arguments. I read that the jury watched the murder video, and I read terrible things about my son, and about myself and my family. Yet I didn't feel personally connected to the case; I felt like a random onlooker reading about a murder trial unrelated to me.

I was feeling very confident that I could successfully fulfil the requirements of a juror now. I felt no emotional connection to it at all. I was definitely in a delusional state. During the days I would absorb all the information I could from the trial and at nights I would process it. Sometimes I would reread things over and over again for clarification. After hearing the abundance of testimony, viewing all the evidence, including the murder video, *1 Lunatic, 1 Icepick,* and closing arguments, the jury received their final instructions from the trial judge on December 15 before being sequestered away. Deliberations would begin the following day. The fate of Luka Magnotta was now in the hands of a jury.

Luka in Prison

That night I thought long and hard about the judge's final instructions. I thought about Luka, I thought about the jury. I was ready to deliberate.

Not knowing when the jury would reach a verdict, I decided I would deliberate as long as I needed to reach my own. For the next several days I ate, slept, and breathed the trial. I reviewed numerous times all the evidence presented in court. I did not consider any outside evidence such as news sources or my own personal connection to the case. I referenced Canada's criminal code and case studies law. I researched the definition of Not Criminally Responsible. Section 16 of the Criminal Code of Canada states:

Defense of mental disorder

No person is criminally responsible for an act committed or an omission made while suffering from a mental disorder that rendered the person incapable of appreciating the nature and quality of the act or omission of knowing that it was wrong.

Presumption

Every person is presumed not to suffer from a mental disorder so as to be exempt from criminal responsibility by virtue of subsection (1), until the contrary is proved on the balance of probabilities.

Burden of proof

The burden of proof that an accused was suffering from a mental disorder so as to be exempt from criminal responsibility is on the party that raises the issue.

Luka had pleaded not guilty to the acts he was accused of but had claimed diminished responsibility due to mental disorders. Luka's lawyer argued that his client was in a psychotic state at the time of the crimes and couldn't be held responsible for his actions. The Crown prosecutor, Louis Bouthillier, argued that the murder was organized and premeditated; and that Luka was purposeful, mindful, and organized; and that he was ultimately responsible for his actions.

The jury heard from sixty-six witnesses from three countries during the twelve-week trial. The jury had four options for a verdict to choose from: guilty of first degree murder, guilty of second degree murder, guilty of manslaughter, or not criminally responsible because of mental disorder. During the trial, Luka chose not to testify.

I considered the following factors when deliberating. Luka admitted to committing the acts. He had no previous history of violence. He reached out for medical help on numerous occasions, but his needs were not properly addressed or dealt with. The police refused to listen to his complaints of being abused. In my opinion he received inadequate legal representation. Political and foreign involvement and media influence, I felt all played a role in the case.

I checked the status of jury deliberation each day and continued to contemplate my own verdict until I was ready to render my decision. On December 21, 2014, I reached my verdict: Not Criminally Responsible on all counts. It was evident that more likely than not during the time of the offenses, Luka Rocco Magnotta was suffering from a mental disorder that rendered him incapable of knowing the acts he committed were wrong. He had suffered terrible abuse at the hands of Manny and was under Manny's complete control. To me, it was obvious he had been in that state of mind for several months.

I was confident that the jury would reach the same conclusion, and I started watching the media coverage again, anxiously awaiting a verdict. It was getting very close to Christmas at that point, but it really didn't feel like Christmastime to me. I rested on Monday, December 22, but on December 23 I decided to go to the mall with my parents and grandchildren to do some very last-minute Christmas shopping. In all honesty, I didn't feel like going anywhere or doing anything, but it was just something I felt I had to do. There were other people to consider, and just like all the other things we had to do to carry on, this was one of them. Life doesn't stop.

The hustle and bustle and spirit of Christmastime was in full swing at the mall, but my mind was elsewhere. I had no feelings of joy that holiday season. All I could think of was the verdict. When is it coming? After shopping for a while, we all sat down to take a break in the comfy chairs in the center of the mall, which was so pretty that time of year with the sparkly holiday decorations and lights. There was Christmas music playing and people were scurrying around doing their last-minute shopping. My little grandbabies were so excited and happy, but I felt empty. I had no Christmas spirit at all.

As we sat there, I overheard some people talking. I heard one say, "They reached a verdict. He's guilty." My heart started pounding. A verdict! I needed to find out what was happening! Suddenly, my phone began to ring nonstop and text messages started pouring in. I ignored them all. I wanted to hear and see for myself what was going on.

People throughout the mall were talking about it, and I could hear bits and pieces of their conversation as I ran to find a media source. I just left my poor family sitting there.

Finally, I was able to learn the details of the verdict, which was reached after eight days of jury deliberation: Guilty of first-degree murder. Life sentence with possibility of parole after twenty-five years. Guilty and maximum sentences for all other charges, nineteen years running concurrently. Juror number nine read the verdict. My knees went weak. I was utterly shocked and devastated.

How could this be? There was no doubt in my mind that my son Luka Magnotta was Not Criminally Responsible! He met the criteria the justice system had in place to determine an NCR verdict in a court of law. I wanted justice, and not just for my son. I felt an NCR conviction would have served justice to all parties involved.

Luka's lawyer filed an appeal with the Quebec Court of Appeal citing judicial error in jury instructions, as well as the verdicts were unreasonable and unsupported by the evidence and the instructions. On February 18, 2015, Luka withdrew his appeal.

12

LUKA

Every time I told Luc LeClair something, it would
mysteriously wind up in the press—Luka Magnotta

It was a weird trial. With a case like this, how could it not
be? It was one of the most bizarre murders in history, why
should the trial be different?

There was never any issue of who did it, just why? It
would be rather hard for Luka to plead not guilty when he
took great pains to provide evidence that he was in fact the
killer.

And there is the rub. Someone that had to do something
like this had to be ridiculously insane, right? If you saw the
video and saw the things that Luka did and don't think Luka
is crazy, well then, you're probably crazy. Everyone knew
Luka killed Jun Lin. He videotaped himself doing it and
posted it on the Internet. I mean, it was him, we all knew
that.

But in the case of this trial, it wasn't that easy. For
the charge of murder, jurors had four ways they could go;
guilty of premeditated first-degree murder; guilty of second-
degree murder; guilty of manslaughter; or not criminally
responsible, which is otherwise known as NCR. There was
zero chance of him being found not guilty, not when he did
what he did, especially not the way he did it.

The judge in the case, Guy Cournoyer, explained
to jurors the concept of NCR saying "Under our law, the
verdict of not criminally responsible by reason of mental
disorder is not a loose term, quite the contrary. There are

specific criteria to determine whether the defense of mental disorder is applicable."

Although he denied it to me, Luka has a long history of professionals saying he is schizophrenic. Many think he also has narcissistic and antisocial personality disorders, and it is easy to see why. But whether or not Luka is mentally ill doesn't have a whole lot to do with the situation when it comes to an NCR defense.

When it comes to Canadian law, suffering from a personality disorder or even schizophrenia isn't enough for an NCR verdict to come down because in theory it doesn't mean Luka didn't understand what he was doing was wrong. What it all boils down to is this. Everyone in the courtroom could think that Luka was the craziest person in the entire world. He could be hearing voices. He could be saying that he was the voice of God; I mean, he could even kill someone, hack his body up, videotape it, and throw the video up on the Internet, (oh wait, he did that) but the only thing that matters is whether or not he understood that killing Jun Lin was not only illegal, but wrong.

And the other thing is, when it comes to Luka, who really knows what he thinks or what moral code he understands? I've interviewed him. I've talked extensively with his mother. I certainly have my ideas of what he thinks, but do I really know what he thinks?

I don't.

He was found guilty of first-degree murder and of all the other charges as well, which consisted of performing indignities on a human corpse, distributing obscene materials, using the postal service to distribute obscene materials, and criminal harassment of Prime Minister Stephen Harper and other members of Parliament. The trial lasted ten weeks, and the jury deliberated eight days, but despite the length of the proceedings, the decision was no real surprise to most. The jury decided Magnotta knew he was doing something wrong when he killed Jun Lin, and the murder was carefully planned and premeditated.

One has to really wonder what our societies definition of "insane" is if Luka's actions didn't fit the definition. Still, he didn't testify at the trial. If he did he might have been able to convince the jury that he was quite psychotic that day. He could have said he heard voices. He could have said that Lin was a government spy. He could have said that Manny told him to do it. He could have said that Manny told him to do everything. Then maybe he could have been asked to, you know, say where Manny lived or what his phone number was or something.

He could have said all sorts of things. But he didn't.

Luka did not play the role of international playboy in court. He had gained weight, wore glasses, sat hunched over and made no eye contact with anyone when the jury was in court. He looked nothing like the fabulous and fascinating person he had attempted to show to the world, with varying degrees of success. When the jury was out of court, his demeanor changed. He became much more animated. He sat up and looked around. Is that because he was attempting to manipulate jurors, or was that because he felt enormous shame around those that were to decide his fate?

Luke LeClair's performance did not receive rave reviews. Sometimes LeClair spoke in English, other times in French. Some media outlets described his performance as bizarre. Once he asked court to be held up because he wanted to go for a walk. His closing arguments lasted but an hour. During them he told the jury to ignore all psychiatric reports, including ones that said that Luka was NCR, and make up their own minds. When he was finished with his summation, he just stopped talking and sat down, leaving the judge to ask him if he was actually done. He was.

Luka told me of LeClair: *He was helpful yet controlling, warm yet abrasive, he worked hard, but on the other hand I did a lot of the work. He infuriated me when he wouldn't let up on the insanity defense. We argued and screamed at each other.*

Prosecutor Louis Bouthillier was a bit more on point. He spent a whole day going through all of the planning that Luka had to go through to kill Jun Lin, including going through every movement Luka made on the surveillance video tapes, the pizza he ordered, the sixteen trips he made back and forth attempting to get rid of the evidence, him going to the post office to mail the body parts, then hitting up a store to buy new sheets. Bouthillier focused on the threatening email Luka sent to journalist Alex West concerning the cat killing videos when Luka said he was soon to be producing a movie that "will have some humans in it, not just pussys." Soon after that a video was posted online showing Luka killing Lin. Not only that there was the infamous video of Magnotta wearing the purple hoodie with an icepick in his hand in which he says, There is apparently a video circulating around the deep web and called *One Lunatic One Ice Pick Video*. Does anyone have a copy of it?" To the prosecutor, all this showed how premeditated this was.

The prosecution also suggested that Luka was just making up symptoms of mental illness to get out of trouble and to escape the situation that he put himself in, which stands in stark contrast to everything Luka told me. They also focused on the fact that while the video that was uploaded doesn't show his face clearly, the unedited footage does. Obviously meaning Luka had attempted to cut out the parts of the video that could identify him. "Sure, Magnotta is narcissistic, but not that narcissistic, I guess," Bouthillier said.

The verdict was unanimous: first-degree murder, which carries a mandatory sentence of twenty-five years in prison with no chance of parole for twenty-five years.

Diran Lin, Jun Lin's father said in a victim statement "I had come to see your trial system to see justice done, and I leave satisfied that you have not let my son down. I had come to learn what happened to my son that night, and I leave without a true or a complete answer. I had come to see remorse, to hear some form of apology, and I leave without anything."

13

*Unfortunately, my lawyer's nonstop insistence
that we go for an NCR defense convinced
me he was the expert—Luka Magnotta*

A system is in place to govern us. We put our trust, faith, health, and sense of justice in the hands of this system. When a part of our system fails one of us (in this case the mental healthcare sector and law enforcement) the legal justice system has to recognize that has happened and not condemn the person who was affected by the failing. That's called damage control, not justice. The system needs to be held accountable for its shortcomings and mistakes like the rest of us have to. My son Luka Magnotta was neglected by the mental healthcare system and law enforcement prior to this. This crime would have been prevented if he had received the proper care when he was screaming for help. In my mind there was no justice served in this case. As a Canadian citizen, I am appalled and ashamed of my country, and as the mother of a wrongly convicted man, I am outraged!

An NCR verdict would not have been a get-out-of-jail-free card for Luka. An NCR verdict would have sent Luka to a psychiatric hospital to receive intense therapy for his mental disorder. He would have been under review yearly by a review board to determine his progress, rehabilitation, and risk to the public. Victims can also attend the review board meetings and give statements. In July of 2013 Bill C-54, the NCR Reform Act, was passed. It imposes mandatory hospitalization times and prolongs review hearings for someone designated as a high-risk NCR offender. 93 percent of NCR patients do not reoffend. Instead they receive effective treatment for their mental illnesses.

Hearing the verdict given to my son was as shocking and painful as it was hearing about this crime for the first time. My heart, soul, and spirit were wounded beyond repair. I spent the next two years trying to recover, getting my mental and physical health stabilized. My feelings, thoughts, and emotions have been all over the map since 2012. I have gone through many stages of grief, shock, anger, dismay, depression, sadness, loss, frustration, shame, betrayal, guilt, blame, fear, regret, and disappointment. I was so confused.

The one and only thing I was sure of was the feeling that never left or changed. Love. I love my son! After many years of professional treatment and therapy, guidance, understanding, and love from my father, I am finally coming to terms with the fact that my son is in prison for first degree murder. But despite this I will never deny my son, and I will never stop loving him no matter what. I will not let this crime define the person he is. My son Luka Magnotta is, was, and always will be a kind, loving, caring, intelligent, resilient, charismatic man. I am proud to be his mother!

There were many lies said during trial. My son Luka was never abused by me, my mother, or my father. He was emotionally and physically abused by his biological father, Don Newman, and by my ex-partner Leo Belanger Sr. I was absolutely shocked and devastated that Luka claimed he had been sexually abused. If this is true, I want to know who did this to him, but Luka has never talked to me about it to this day.

My three older children were satisfactorily homeschooled according to the provincial guidelines, and then they were successfully integrated into the public school system. This is not that odd. All sorts of people from many different backgrounds homeschool their children.

I was in two very abusive relationships for almost thirty years combined. I was physically and emotionally abused by both Don Newman and Leo Belanger Sr. All my children grew up living in these unhealthy, dysfunctional conditions. I will always live with regret and guilt for what my children went through; I wish I had been strong enough, brave enough, and smart enough back then to break free and get us all out sooner than I did. I admit I drank, but I was not an alcoholic. I also was suffering from mental health issues years ago that went undiagnosed until a few years ago.

I want my children to know that I take full responsibility and ownership for all my mistakes and shortcomings as a mother that have directly or indirectly affected them. Excuses, reasons or explanations won't change anything. I am truly and sincerely sorry for anything and everything I ever did or said that hurt any one of them.

I am so thankful that I have loving, happy, healthy relationships with each of them now. I love them with all my heart. I am very proud to be their mother.

I have spent the last few years thinking constantly about what could have happened to my son. My son Luka came from an abusive, dysfunctional, sheltered environment. He suffered from a mental disorder starting in his late teens. He improperly and inconsistently took his prescribed medication, but he had minimal substance abuse. In his early years, he was shy and inward; as a teen to adult he became outgoing and confident. Although he dropped out of high school, he is extremely intelligent, his IQ score is 138. He did not hold a steady job. He moved and travelled a lot. He lived primarily on his own since his late teens. His sexual orientation is homosexual. He was very private and secretive. He lied and has been distant from his family at times. He got involved with people with whom he trusted and befriended quickly. They took advantage of him because of his kind, trusting nature. He was let down many times by people he considered friends. He became extremely paranoid and thought he was always in danger from others. He had a nonviolent criminal record. He tried but never really seemed to fit in comfortably anywhere. When the world he lived in had let him down time after time and hurt him he started to create a perfect life for himself, one that he could control, a life that he wished for. He inserted the perfect, people, places, and things into his new world and tried to convince himself and others that he was happy. Then his perfect world began to fall apart. Luka was in a constant inner battle, as if he was being taken over by something or someone. I witnessed these painful changes in my son over the years.

My son Luka tried hard to cope and deal with his mental disorder. He struggled and battled for many years. He was even hospitalized a few times, but once he stabilized he was released and on his own again. Follow-up and monitoring of mentally ill patients should be mandatory if they have been hospitalized, if their families have serious concerns (not just if they are a threat to themselves or others), or if they are involved in criminal activity. No matter how insignificant a crime seems, it's a red flag and a cry for help. Once a person reaches the age of eighteen, it's almost impossible to get involved and intervene unless they are a threat to themselves or others. Many mentally ill people do not fall under that category and still desperately need someone to step in and facilitate for them.

Luka never fell under that category until he was accused of the cat-killing videos. Even though he was exhibiting strange, bizarre, and unusual behaviors prior, that wasn't enough for intervention. Over the years I had contacted his psychiatrist many times with my concerns and observations, but there wasn't much I could do unless Luka cooperated. He couldn't be forced to see the doctor or take his medication. He wasn't in the right frame of mind to know what was in his best interests or to follow through with a mental health care plan. When we learned of the cat-killing videos, we fully cooperated with the authorities. We wanted them to find Luka, arrest him, and bring him in to get medical treatment. We knew this was getting really bad and out of control, and it was going to get worse if he didn't get help. I wish they had of caught him then. If they did a life would have been saved, and Luka would have gotten help and been able to completely explain what was going on with controlling, abusive Manny. It was extremely difficult to keep tabs on Luka when he started travelling out of province and out of Canada. It took days to find him when there was an international manhunt for him.

As a result of this tragedy and to set a good example for my children and grandchildren, I have addressed my own mental health issues. I sought out medical help in 2012, and I am not ashamed to share the findings. I have been formally diagnosed with depression, anxiety, bipolar disorder, compound trauma, PTSD, OCD, and panic attacks. I have also been diagnosed with anemia, cardiac dysrhythmia, high blood pressure, and vertigo. I take my prescribed medications daily to manage my illnesses, and I see my doctor, psychotherapist, and psychiatrist regularly and my clinical therapist when needed.

I have good days, and I have bad days. I have many days when I am full of energy and could take on the world (manic). Then I crash, and I don't feel like doing anything at all (depression). I will ride the waves of mental illness for the rest of my life, but I won't let them pull me under. I keep my head above water and keep telling myself that I am in control. I try hard not to let my mental and physical illnesses interfere with life. I find solace these days in writing, painting, drawing, country drives, boating with my father, fishing, and rock collecting. I talk to the water (it relaxes me immensely), I listen to my eighties tunes, I enjoy spending time with my children and grandchildren. I practice martial arts; I have a black belt in karate and several years of kung fu training; I advocate for many prisoners. enjoy cooking, and I occasionally bake when I'm really stressed out.

I hope that by sharing my personal struggle with mental health that has affected my life for many years and my son's painful, catastrophic struggle with the mental health system and law enforcement that resulted in a death and a life sentence in prison helps someone. I hope my story can spare a struggling, mentally ill person, or a family struggling with mental illness the pain and suffering I've endured. I hope that my story enlightens and educates not only the public, but the mental health system, law enforcement, and the judicial system as well. A tragedy such as ours was preventable. The healthcare system, law enforcement, and our judicial system failed my son miserably! I have a voice, and I intend to use it! My goal is to make changes to the many flawed sectors of our overall failing system.

While working on my manuscript for this book I became overwhelmed. I missed Luka so much. It had been three years since we had spoken to each other. I had taken the past three years to process everything, get professional help and get stronger. I felt I was in a better place now and ready to see him. I had never stopped loving him.

I wondered if he even wanted to see me ever again. There was only one way for me to find out. I decided to contact Port-Cartier institution where my son is being housed and request a visitation application. I didn't write my son to tell him about my intentions, as I didn't really know what to say to him in a letter. I love him dearly, and I longed for him to be part of my life again. I had a deep, empty feeling, like a part of me was missing. My son was that part; I needed my son. Over the next several days I stayed in frequent contact with the prison's visitation correspondent. I asked several questions as to how the visiting process works. When I received the application I filled it out and returned it via email, and I sent the two requested photos of myself via regular mail. As I took the photos to the post office, I felt really good about it all, taking the first step to seeing Luka again had happened.

Luka and Anthony Jolin in Prison

Once I received my approval letter, I was able to book a visit, so I called the prison, made an appointment, and asked them to please let Luka know I was coming. I was travelling a long way to see him, and I wanted to make sure that he wanted to see me. It would have crushed me if he didn't. The correspondent said he would send a message to Luka and get back to me. I was very excited, but nervous.

That day, I got out my photo albums and started going through them. I found so many old photos of Luka. I spread them out on the floor and reminisced. Those photos brought back so many happy memories with my son. I could actually look at all those photos now and remember the good times — so many good times — and feel happy. I lost track of time that day. I looked at those photos and some old cards and letters for several hours. I felt so content. As I was putting away the albums, I was thinking about all the different scenarios that might occur surrounding the visit. I thought about what it would feel like for us both when we saw each other again. I thought about how Luka would be affected by seeing me again. I wondered if he would be willing to talk about what happened and answer some of my questions. I wondered what he looked like now. I imagined how wonderful it would feel to hug him again! I thought about how sad I'll be when I have to leave him and how he would feel when we had to say goodbye. I thought about him being alone in prison to process all this.

I stayed busy and positive; I started planning the trip to Port-Cartier, Quebec. It was going to be a long road trip. It was over 1,300 miles to the prison from where I lived in Peterborough, Ontario. I got out the maps and went online, searched a travel route, and looked up accommodations. I also searched Port-Cartier and correctional services websites for visitor information. I even took a virtual tour of a federal prison. Preparing for the trip made me feel good, like this was something really happening, and it kept my mind busy.

I pushed the thought of Luka possibly not wanting to see me right out of my head. Why did I even think that in the first place? Of course he wanted to see me! I made appointments to see both my doctor and therapist to have them on board with my plans. They both offered me really great advice, and I had both their blessings and support. My boyfriend at the time was accompanying me on this trip, which I really appreciated. He offered to rent us a car and do all the driving as well. The trip was estimated to be about a fourteen-hour drive from where we were. Everything was in place for my long journey. I was going to be reunited with my son in a couple of days! When I went to bed that night, I was elated. I was so proud of myself. I had come such a long way. It wasn't that I hadn't seen Luka because of what had happened, it was more that it had taken so much out of me. I was now actually strong enough and well enough to be able to be part of my son's life. I was healing. I fell asleep that night feeling at peace with myself, a feeling I had not had in a very long time.

Once we were on the road, I called the prison. They told me they had given my message to Luka; he knew I was coming. I told them, "Great, I'm on my way to see him!"

We arrived in the remote little town of Port-Cartier at 8:30 a.m. on Wednesday morning; we had been driving for nineteen hours. My visit started in half an hour. We quickly checked into Le Q'artier Hotel so I could freshen up. The hotel was literally only five minutes away from the prison. We jumped back into the car and headed over. There was a spectacular waterfall near the road that led down to the prison. admired it as we drove past. Water is my element; it has a very tranquil effect on me. As we turned onto the last stretch of road before the prison, my heart began to beat faster. After all that had happened being so close to my son was a surreal experience. I was so excited.

We pulled up into the prison compound with five minutes to spare until my visit was to begin. We were immediately greeted by two swiftly moving black SUVs carrying heavily armed guards. They questioned us as to why we were on the property and why we had stopped in an authorized-vehicle-only driveway. I explained that I was here to visit an inmate and that I was confused as to where to go. I identified myself and informed them who I was there to visit. The guards instructed me to go through the gate and into the main building. My boyfriend was told to leave the property as he had not been cleared to visit. He was however allowed to come back and pick me up at the time my visit was over if he waited for me in the designated pick-up area. I got out of the car and started walking over to the building. I felt wide-awake now after our encounter with the 'welcoming committee' in spite of having only two hours sleep since we left Ontario. I noticed how eerily quiet it was. It made me wonder how many people came to visit the inmates there, as it was a very secluded place.

I was getting really anxious. I entered the building and went up to the security window and announced my arrival. I presented my photo identification to the guard and told him who I was there to see. He welcomed me and passed me a visitor sign-in sheet through the slot in the security window. After I had signed he made a few phone calls. He spoke French, so all I could understand was the word "Magnotta." I waited patiently — no, impatiently — for several minutes. I took in my surroundings as I waited. The front section of the building was cordoned off from the office/security check portion of the building by a large tinted security window. From where I was standing I could vaguely see the guards behind the glass. There were several of them; they had a clear view of the entrance to the prison compound. The area where I was waiting was very small. The outside door led into it; there were two chairs and a wall of small lockers. Through the windows I could see and hear the office area guards. They were speaking French amongst themselves. Although I don't speak or understand French, I could tell they were engaging in pleasant conversation, which calmed me a bit. A guard came in through the office area and out to where I was standing. He introduced himself to me and informed me that he was assigned to accompany me on my first visit. I had never been to a federal prison before. I didn't know their security procedures or what to expect, except for what I had read about on the prison website. It was very comforting for me to have the guard with me; he was very pleasant and helpful. It is amazing what small kindnesses can mean in a situation such as this.

He explained the process to me as we went along. He helped me open a locker, so I could put all my personal belongings inside. Visitors are not permitted to have any outside items with them, including jewelry, though you're allowed to take your locker key with you. He led the way into the first security screening area. I walked through a body scanner, then up to a locked turnstile where I was given a security card attached to a bungee cord. I was instructed to tap the card on the indicated area to unlock the turnstile.

My assigned guard asked me to proceed to the room directly in front of me; another guard was on his way into that room. My guard asked me to step into that room and stop inside the yellow dotted-lined box area on the floor. He stood directly behind me. The other guard was standing beside the table with some sort of drug-scanning equipment. He grabbed a pair of purple latex gloves from a box and put them on. I thought, Oh no! What the hell, am I going to be strip-searched? My guard quickly assured me that I was just going to be wanded to see if they could detect any traces of drugs on me. That was a relief. I was handed a long, black wand with a small piece of fabric secured to the end. I was told to rub the top of the wand up and down the surfaces of my pants and shirt. The guard led me out of that building and across the courtyard to the second building. On the way, he prepared me for the next security phase. The canine search. The guard asked me if I was afraid of dogs. I like dogs, but I am cautious of them. I replied, "No, I'm good."

We entered the second building, which was a large room with a security window area, a few doors, and a wooden chair sitting in the middle of the floor. He told me that another guard would be joining us shortly with a drug detector dog. He just got those words out of his mouth when I heard the dog's claws tapping on the floor behind one of the doors. I could hear his handler's voice as he spoke sternly to the dog in French.

The door opened and out came a very large dog along with a very large guard. My guard stepped back and told me to follow the instructions of the other guard who entered the room with the dog. The guard asked me in a thick French accent if I was okay with dogs; I said yes. He told me to take a seat in the chair, put my hands on my knees, to sit still, and not to interact with the dog. "The dog will walk around you and sniff you. He may put his paws up on you." I sat down in the chair, and he unleashed the dog and voiced his commands in French. He told me he would not let the dog harm me. I thought to myself, Well, that's a relief and very encouraging to know! As I sat there, the dog sniffed my hands, legs, and arms; then he went around to the back of the chair. The guard stayed close and circled around with the dog. All of a sudden, I felt the dog sniffing in my hair. He was up on his hind legs with his front paws on the back of my chair. I could hear him panting, and I could feel his breath on the back of my neck. I started freaking out. What the hell was this dog doing? I got scared, I thought he might bite me! The guard yelled out another command, and the dog jumped down. The guard said, "It's okay, stand up now, the dog will circle around you and sniff you again." The dog circled around and sniffed me again for a minute or so. Then the guard called him back, and he hooked him back on the leash. He said, "Okay, you're good. Thank you," and they left.

My guard said, "This way please." We then waited by a big metal door. Soon he called out to the guards behind the security glass to unlock it. It buzzed and clicked; he motioned for me to continue through, but I could not pull it open — it was too heavy. He said, "Allow me," and he pulled it open. Once we were through, the door locked behind us. On the other side of the door there was a hallway; we stopped for a minute while he pointed out the washroom to me. He said if I needed to use it during my visit, they would let me out to do so. In front of us there was a small, high-up room with a big security window. Inside that room, there were two or three very heavily armed guards; rifles were visible. We were let into a door, which locked behind us. We were now in between three doors. One we had just come through, one they bring the inmate through, and one leading into the visiting room. He told me that my son was in that room waiting for me. My heart started to beat fast with anticipation, and I could feel my face getting warm. I had not seen him in so long, and now my son was literally only a few feet away from me. I heard the click of the door.

The guard said, "Go on in; your son is sitting at the far table on the left." I opened the door and walked inside, the guard right behind me.

And there he was. The guard motioned to Luka that is was okay to come and greet me. I was overwhelmed with happiness as we both made our way across the room to each other! As we got closer we both opened our arms. I had been waiting years to hug my son again, and it was finally going to happen! Luka had the biggest, warmest smile on his face as he reached out and wrapped his arms around me. I wrapped my arms around him, put my head on his chest, and closed my eyes. I was completely consumed by love. An overpowering sense of peace came over me.

In this realm time stood still and in that moment of frozen time in the arms of my son, I elevated to a higher plane of consciousness and felt the power of insight envelop me. It felt as if I was experiencing pinnacle clarity. I moved through multi-dimensions of time and space with a vast awareness and understanding of my life. I acquired the ability to heal, and I discovered closure. I came away from that experience with a greater purpose of being. The invaluable knowledge I obtained during that epiphany will sustain me for the rest of my life.

My son looked amazing, healthy, in great shape, and happy. We took a seat at a little round visiting table and held hands. Unshaken by the presence of heavily armed guards, we spent the next two hours baring our souls to each other. My son welcomed me back into his life with open arms. I came back to the prison that afternoon, went through the same security procedures again, and visited with my son for another two hours. We have a bond that will never be broken, and the love we have together will last forever; it will stand the test of time and prevail. We are related by chance, but we love each other and stay together by choice. Because of chance and choice, I have a son in my life whom I adore. I will stand by him, support, and protect him as long as there is breath in my body. We continue to stay in contact. We talk on the phone every day and write to each other. I go to visit him as often as possible, and I will be there for him whenever he needs me.

The man that sat before me and talked with me at Port-Cartier Federal Institution is a level-headed, coherent, honest, loving, empathetic, and gentle person. He has fought very hard over the past several years to break free and save himself. He came back to be the person he really is. I am proud of him for finding the strength and courage to fight his way back from the hardest battle of his life.

As we talked I asked Luka, why he didn't speak to Jun Lin's father? What I took away from that conversation was that Luka considered the Lin family's feelings and felt that no matter what he said it would cause further pain to them, so he didn't say anything at all; he did not want to cause them any more grief. How do you apologize for something like this? Saying sorry doesn't change it. I am very glad Luka didn't speak to Jun Lin's father or his family. He's right. It would have been painful for them to have heard anything he had to say. If the circumstances were reversed, no apology or explanation would make me feel better or otherwise. It would only open the door for me to verbally attack back and that wouldn't change anything. At the beginning of this tragic ordeal, I felt it was imperative that Luka give answers to the Lin family. I've since changed my mind. In my opinion being silent was the most respectful thing for Luka to do. Many people who followed this case and the trial took Luka's silence as a lack of empathy and remorse on his part. The public was quick to come to that conclusion and assume the worst from him. Everyone including Luka knows that an apology and/or a statement counts for something in a court of law. I believe Luka risked being judged and ridiculed rather than inflicting any more pain and suffering on the Lin family.

14

I explained the doctor made a bad diagnosis.
Sometimes it happens—Luka Magnotta

Police profilers didn't feel that they were looking at a lust murder, which would mean in essence that Luka was taken over by darkest carnal desires and acted out of some warped sense of passion. Instead they had a very strong belief that the murder and the video itself were planned, and that the acts that Luka committed during the murder had already been thought out and were presented for effect.

In essence profilers felt that Luka was not only the director and the screenwriter of the film he made, but he even acted in it, behaving in a rather theatrical way throughout. He wasn't doing all of these horrific things to Jun Lin's corpse because he was driven to do so, whether it be by insanity or depraved lust, he was just following a script, and trying to win an Oscar for Best Actor in the process.

Their opinion was that he killed Lin and defiled his corpse because he wanted to provoke, that he wanted to get a reaction, which he certainly did. One wonders what the endgame was of all of this. Didn't he know that there was no going back from this? That he had gone too far?

And why? Was he just empty inside in a way that most of us couldn't imagine, and this would be a way he would fill that hole? Was getting attention for being a total psycho better than getting no attention at all?

Profilers thought he might have a narcissistic personality. That he wanted others to notice him, to know who he was.

While the killing obviously had the trappings of something inspired by paraphilias, ones that are inspired by the sickest type of sexual desire one could imagine. It all seemed to be just for show. There was no sign he had an erection in the video, even when he simulated sex with the corpse, Luka had his pants on. It seemed it was all just to shock his millions of viewers, his new fans. This is interesting in itself, as the only thing that might be more disturbing than a man killing and dismembering another man because they are driven sexually to do so, is someone that is just pretending that they are.

Watts said his diagnosis of schizophrenia "is based on Mr. Magnotta's clear and well-documented history of suffering from delusions, hallucinations, disorganized speech, and prominent negative symptoms such as affective flattening (diminished emotional expression). Mr. Magnotta has suffered for many years from delusional beliefs that he was being followed, watched and that people were trying to harm or kill him. At times he has experienced thought broadcasting and feeling his mind and emotions were under external control. Throughout the course of his illness and particularly during his acute psychotic decompensations, Mr. Magnotta's delusions have been accompanied by auditory hallucinations of multiple individuals calling him names, making homophobic slurs and instructing him to either harm himself or harm others. These symptoms have caused significant social and occupational dysfunction since the onset of his illness in the late 1990's. For example, he was unable to work and was sufficiently impaired to obtain Ontario Disability Support Program payments for several years and was offered this several times by his doctors."

Was Luka mentally ill? He told me he was not, that he never once has been ill. Not in his life.

Luka has said that the first time he ever went to see a psychiatrist was when his grandmother became worried about him. She thought he was on drugs. That would have been much easier to deal with than the reality of the situation. Luka said that at the time he was feeling scared and that he was hearing things. His grandmother said he was talking really loudly. He was diagnosed with schizophrenia at that time.

When Dr. Watts asked if he had a lot of episodes like that later in life Luka said that if he did that he tried to block things like that out, that he didn't like thinking of the fact that he had a psychiatric diagnosis because he was afraid people would leave him. It embarrassed him. He didn't want people to think he was crazy. He wouldn't tell friends about it nor would he tell clients about it when he was doing sex work because he didn't want them to think he was weird. Luka always wanted to be cool, not weird.

Sometimes he would hear voices talking to him; other times he would feel enormous panic. He said at times he would feel that the soul of Marilyn Monroe was inside of him "because she had a lot of sex; when I dress up as her, sometimes I feel like she is making me more beautiful, I have a connection with her because of her childhood, I love her so much." He wanted very much to be her.

Once he felt that someone in the government was watching him because he had printed out information about Aldrich Ames and Robert Hanssen, notorious Cold War spies. The belief that the government was following him came and went over the years. In 2007 it was particularly strong. He thought that his phone was being bugged and that he had to move every few months to keep one step ahead of them. He thought he was being spied on, and the government was tracking his movements.

He first applied for ODSP, which is a Canadian version of Disability, at the age of 18. On the application his psychiatrist noted that Luka was hearing voices and having visual hallucinations as well. He was withdrawn and anxious, and was taking antipsychotic medications. At the time Luka said that he often wouldn't leave home due to fears that people were watching him and wanted to kill him. He also complained of hearing voices in his head telling him to hurt himself.

He was hospitalized in 2003 for psychiatric reasons. When he was discharged it was noted that once again Luka was hearing voices, and they were making him very anxious. When he was admitted to the hospital, he became frightened and swore at his hallucinations. He also talked of people watching him saying, "It's not fair, why is this happening to me?"

Early in his life when he lived in a group home, he thought the other clients were jealous of him. He once stated that his father was jealous of him as well "because I'm going to be a celebrity, a superstar."

He told one doctor that people were trying to destroy his modeling career by putting photos of him on the Internet. He thought people were stalking him. He heard voices that said he walked like an ape. He kept his curtains drawn at home because if he didn't people would try and take his picture through the windows. He moved often because he was being followed.

When Luka moved back to Toronto in 2011, people were looking for him because of the kitten video. Groups were pushing for him to be arrested, he was getting death threats. He couldn't concentrate. People actually *were* watching him and following him. He felt too anxious to drive. He heard voices that told him to kill himself. He hated to go outside of his apartment. Sometimes he would yell at the voices and tell them to leave him alone. He thought his neighbors looked at him oddly because of all the yelling. He was lonely and would sometimes meet men on Craigslist to hook up with them. He couldn't get a job. He thought it might be because of his reputation on the Internet. Who would want to hire a cat killer that was banging Karla Homolka after all? It wasn't the best of resumes.

People would constantly threaten him on Twitter and Facebook because of the cat videos. Strangers would look at him, and he would think they were planning to kill him. The voices got louder. They called him a faggot. They said he was stupid.

When he was hospitalized in Miami, his admission diagnosis was "Psychosis, Not Otherwise Specified." The Miami Beach Police had brought him to the hospital in a confused state. He said that he couldn't remember how he got to Miami or how long he had been there.

And what of Manny? I am sure he could shed some light on all of this. If only anyone knew who he was and where he is?

Luka wonders why people aren't looking for Manny. *Why didn't the police search for people's names such as Manny Lopez and others? They responded they "didn't believe others were involved. When asked how they knew I had eighty accounts online they said, "This info was sent to us." They couldn't provide any proof because there was none.*

I have studied psychology thoroughly it has become an invaluable tool for me, so I am able to analyze situations very effectively and respond accordingly. As was widely reported but very inaccurate I have no mental disorders, I never have in the past either. I do not take any medications, period. In my early years I was misdiagnosed and this diagnosis followed me. I have explained this to each doctor I visited over the years. The original doctor misdiagnosed both my father and myself. Every doctor afterwards couldn't understand this bizarre opinion. My family jokes with my father and I about it, it's ridiculous and we all just laugh at the absurdity.

There is nothing wrong with me in any clinical sense. My entire life I've never taken medication. I actually think society is extremely sick. For example, on the plane back three detectives were arguing nonstop about whom would be seen walking me out. They almost had a fist fight.

I was going through a lot of severe abuse in New York City from a lover, Manny Lopez. This individual was involved in a lot of underground and shady activities. Romeo Salta, my New York attorney, has all the documentation on Manny. The people who know me, know him, and our history understand what happened and the abuse I suffered.

Luka met Manny online. At first Manny was nice. He and Luka were friends. Friends that fucked a lot.

Manny liked to tie Luka up when they fucked. Sex would get rough at times, a little too rough for Luka's liking, but Manny would always be cool. He would always stop when Luka would say the agreed upon safe word.

As time went on he wasn't so nice. Sometimes when Manny was getting off, he would punch Luka in the head. He wanted to tape himself fucking Luka and would often ask Luka to do a threesome with him, so Manny could put it on the Internet and make money.

Sometimes Luka thought he didn't want to see Manny anymore, but when he tried to not hang out as much, Manny would tell him he knew a lot of powerful people in the government and would insinuate he would get back at Luka somehow. He knew things about Luka from the Internet, He knew that he liked Marilyn Monroe. Manny talked a lot about Rikers prison, he made it sound like if anyone found out Luka was an escort, he could send him there. Luka couldn't leave Manny; he had no choice.

He took Luka's medications away. According to Manny Scientology was where it was at. The medications would just make him want to kill himself. He didn't need them. Luka liked Scientology because of Tom Cruise. Manny told Luka the only reason he felt fucked up was because of his medications, but Luka said he needed meds to be stable. If he got off them he got paranoid, he heard voices. Sometimes when he said things like this, Manny punched him in the face.

Luka was afraid of Manny. He thought if he moved to Florida maybe he could get away from him. He changed his phone number, but somehow Manny found it and called him. Manny told Luka he was sorry. He wouldn't call Luka names anymore. He would stop punching him in the head.

At one point Manny asked Luka out to dinner, Luka thought that was really nice of him to do. Then he told him he had a surprise for him. He had a storage bag with him and a vacuum cleaner. He wanted to make a "Crush" video. He said those were super popular right now. Crushing animals. Killing them. He wanted Luka to kill his cats. They could film it and put it on the Internet. It would make a lot of money.

Luka said "No, it will make me sick."

But Manny said that he had to make the video. If Luka didn't make it, he might get punched, or Manny might put him in Rikers, or maybe Manny would call immigration officials. Something bad would happen.

The day of the first kitten video, Manny was talking on the telephone and just kept walking in and out of the room, in and out, in and out. He had a bunch of videos he has taken of himself pissing on Luka, which terrified him. What if he made them public? What then?

When it was time to kill the kittens, Luka hesitated but Manny said, "Come on, come on." He seemed really mad. He showed Luka how to set up the camera. He didn't have all day. Time is money after all. Luka was terrified. His mind was racing. He tried to stall but Manny said, "Just fucking do it."

Manny was in the hallway when Luka suffocated the cats. Then Manny took pictures of him rubbing the dead cats on his balls.

Luka cried.

These are things Manny forced Luka to do: He made him drink alcohol, smoke marijuana, drink his urine, and eat his feces. He forced him to eat animal parts and to have sex with dogs and cats.

These are things Manny did to Luka: He strangled him, cut him with a knife, cut him with his keys, spit on him, raped him, and told him that if he went to any doctors he would kill him.

No one has been able to find any proof that Manny exists, not even by knowing friends or relatives of his. Does anyone know where to find Manny Lopez?

15

*Society needs to realize that the majority of the time
inmates do not worry about other inmates, it's the staff
and the guards that are the issue—Luka Magnotta*

In December 2016, my son and I began the lengthy process
of applying for and being considered to participate in the
Private Family Visit (PFV) program through Correctional
Services Canada (CSC), which means that I would have the
opportunity to spend time alone with Luka, for the first time in
many years. This is a program where family members apply
to the institution and the inmate makes a request through
their parole officer. CSC requires all participating family
members to do a lengthy interview with a parole officer
in their community. Inmates are eligible if they have been
following their correctional plan, and they demonstrated
good behavior. Once the assessments are in and eligibility
is determined, the warden, visiting committee, and parole
officer have a meeting together and make a decision. An
available PFV date is chosen and booked. The duration of
the visit is usually seventy-two hours. PFVs have to take
place on the weekends starting Friday morning through to
Monday morning. We were granted a ninety-six hour visit
because we were coming from out of Province.

The point of the program is to encourage inmates to
develop and maintain family and community ties and
prepare them for their return to the community. While the
visits are long, either the inmate or the family member can
stop the visit at any time. A phone is in the unit solely for

direct calls with institution staff and does not allow outgoing calls. All items that family members bring for their PFV are up to the institution's discretion as to whether they will be allowed into the PFV unit. Prohibited items were listed on the CSC website, and any items not permitted would be held in a locker for the family members until the visit is over. Violence or committing a crime are not tolerated and are punishable by law. In the application it asks to state if you require medication, what kind, dose, and frequency. Medication is not permitted in the unit. Provisions are in place for taking it. I take prescribed medication five times per day.

There were a lot of things we weren't sure of, for example we were never even given a time to arrive at the institution. I had to call to find out. It was very unsettling not knowing fully what to expect, but I was still excited.

I had concerns about this visit from the get-go. My father was ill and I would have no communication with him (except in an emergency). I notified Port-Cartier staff that I had given my father the institution's phone number, but I worried about whether he would be able to get through to me, because of the language barrier, as they mostly spoke French at the prison I would have no contact with my other children as well as I was not allowed to use my cellphone, and this troubled me. I didn't know the procedure I would have to go through for taking my medication. I smoke, and I would not be permitted to do so for the entire visit.

When I decided I wanted to do a PFV back in December 2016, there were two main reasons. I really wanted to be able to spend as much time as possible with Luka, as I missed him very much, and I wanted to tell him that I wrote a book. I didn't feel that it was appropriate to tell him about my book during a normal visit, over the phone, or in a letter. I needed to tell him in person in a private setting and have the time to discuss with him my reasons for writing the book you are reading now. I did not know how he was going to take my news.

Also, since resuming contact with Luka in October after being apart for three years, we still had a lot of catching up to do. We talk on the phone every day, and we exchange letters, but this visit would be the most amount of time I've spent with Luka in ten years. I was incredibly happy about this despite my concerns. Our visit was booked for Friday, April 21, 2017, through Tuesday, April 25, 2017.

My boyfriend at the time, and I set out on Wednesday, April 19, for the long road trip to Port-Cartier. We hoped to arrive by Thursday afternoon, so we would have time to rest up before our visit. Luka phoned me several times along the way. We were both so excited and happy that we were going to see each other soon. It had been quite a while since my boyfriend had seen Luka, and they were both looking forward to their reunion. Besides talking on the phone and writing letters, it had been probably eight years since they had seen each other in person.

We arrived in Port-Cartier on Thursday, April 20 as planned. We rested up that evening, and Luka and I talked on the phone before we turned in for the night. He was so glad that we had arrived safely and that we were so close to him. We got up bright and early the next morning and headed over to the institution, a five-minute car ride from the hotel. Upon arriving we parked in the designated visitor's parking area grabbed our weekend luggage and headed to the main security building. I had butterflies in my stomach. I was excited but nervous about what the check-in process would entail for a PFV. We entered the building to begin our weekend stay in a federal prison.

We were greeted by CSC guards at the reception window who told us to wait for visitation staff to come for us. Two visitation department staff members entered the office area and instructed us to put our jewelry, cell phones, car keys, purse, wallet, and medication into the tiny assigned locker and bring the key, which would fit assigned locker #2 in the next building.

The two guards escorted us out of the main building, across the courtyard, and into the second building. We were brought into the visitation room, which was the same room I had visited Luka in during my last visit. The guards instructed us to take all our belongings out of our bags and put them on the top basket/rack-type shelf on the trolley. For all creams, shampoos, conditioners, and products not in see-through or sealed containers, we were instructed to squeeze as much as you would need into sterile specimen bottles that they provided. These were the same containers used for collecting urine samples.

Once we were finished there we were escorted out the door and across the courtyard to the PFV unit. I was so surprised when they directed us toward it as we had passed by it earlier while going into the second building, and I didn't take notice of it. There were three, ground-level units with small front yards. The units were separated by cement walls. The entire three-unit area was surrounded by tall barbed wire fencing, and each unit had a large, steel-barred gate with a large built-in locking mechanism that required a very large key to unlock. The guards unlocked the gate to the middle PFV unit, "click," we walked through, then "CLANG." As they walked us up the walkway it reminded me of a hotel from the outside. It had a sliding glass/screen door, and in the corner was a regular front door with no lock.

I walked into the entrance way, then stepped around the corner into the living room/kitchen open-concept area, and there was Luka waiting for us, I was so surprised, as they hadn't told us that he would already be there. He looked amazing. He gave my boyfriend and me a big hug. I hugged him for a very long time. I was so glad to be there with him, I missed him so much!

Before the guards left they showed us where the direct line phone was. We could use the phone at any time for assistance, and we would be using it at my medication times, so they could come to the unit and take me to the main building to take my medication. They also informed us that they would be checking in on us approximately four to five times daily. They would phone; we would pick up; they would then say, "Come to the door," and a minute later guards would come to the fence, and we all have to wave and be accounted for.

The PFV unit exceeded my expectations. It was very nice and felt like being in an apartment. Luka gave us the grand tour. The living room had a big couch and TV with cable, a VCR, and movies. The kitchen had a nice table with four chairs and placemats. The kitchen was fully stocked with dishes, pots, pans, bakeware, and food, which Luka had to order and pay for two weeks in advance. Inmates are responsible for paying for the weekend food with their own money.

Luka then took us down the hall to show us the bedrooms. They were both modestly furnished and decorated. Luka insisted we stay in the larger of the two bedrooms. At the end of the hall was a stacking washer/dryer combo for our use during our visit. Another large bin full of clean linen, towels, sheets, blankets, and facecloths was in the hallway for us to use. There was a large bathroom at the end of the hall too. It had a sink, toilet, bathtub and shower, storage shelves, and a wall mirror. The unit had several pleasant wall hangings throughout. It was quite a surprise to me. I never expected our visit would take place in such a spacious and comfortable place. Two freshly baked loaves of bread, which were baked at the institution's kitchen, were left on the counter for us. One of the guards came by and brought us some extra things, like peanut butter, herbs, and soup mix. A few of the guards were exceptionally nice, pleasant, friendly, and hospitable; although, most I would encounter were rude and nosey, had bad attitudes, and made me feel very uncomfortable there.

The feeling of being confined behind gates and barbed wire fences with sensors all around was hard to get used to. I was completely out of my element. I'd never had an experience like this before. I tried not to look outside and just focused on spending good quality, happy time with Luka. I loved being there with him, he makes me laugh, he's kind, and he's a great conversationalist. We all sat down at the kitchen table and talked for hours, and it was wonderful. We cooked some lunch together and chatted some more. Inmates are allowed to purchase a disposable camera, so Luka brought one for the visit. After lunch we had fun taking some pictures.

That evening I had to take my medication. Luka picked up the direct line phone and informed security that his mother was ready to take her medication (Luka speaks French). Before long four female guards arrived to pick me up. The steel gate was unlocked for me to exit "click" – "CLANG." All four guards never spoke a word to me on our way over to the main building. They were speaking in French amongst themselves. Even laughing at times. I could tell they were talking about me (us). They made me feel very uncomfortable. I was taken into the main building, through the body scanner, and out the door to my locker where my medication was stored. I was given a paper cup for water. One of the female guards stood in front of me with her arms crossed while I took out my medication. I opened the washroom door to get some water, and before the door had a chance to close, she banged it open with her boot and watched me fill the cup with water. I came out of the washroom, sat down on the chair, opened my pill bottle, took out my pill, and swallowed it in front of her. I put my medication and paper cup back in my locker and locked it up.

The other female guards were in the office area waiting for us. I could see them through the window. They were still talking and laughing and looking my way. I could not believe how rude and unprofessional these women were! The four of them escorted me back to the PFV unit, opened the steel gate, and locked me back in. I felt like a caged circus sideshow because of them. There was no reason to have four guards show up to take me for my medication. They all wanted to come for their own curiosity and amusement o see the mother of the famous inmate Luka Magnotta.

I shared my first medication pick-up experience with Luka and my boyfriend. Luka was not surprised. He said this sort of behavior from most of the guards is an everyday thing there. He said that they are extremely rude and do what they want. Luka hugged me and said, "Are you okay sweetie?" I was okay but, I still didn't like how I was just treated by those guards. And I had to do this three more times that night. Three more med pick-ups. We carried on with our evening. We all had so much catching up to do. Luka and I decided to make dessert, so we baked a lovely banana cake. It was so nice to be able to cook and bake with my son again. It was something we used to do quite often. My last three evening med pick-ups were much better. Different guards came every time. Most of them were very polite and friendly or respectfully quiet and professional. But I knew the reason different guards were coming every time. They all wanted to see Luka Magnotta's mother. When it was time to go to bed, it felt so good to be able to give Luka a hug before bed and have him sleep in the room right next to me.

I had to stop myself from tip-toeing into his room and tucking him in while he was sleeping like I used to when he was a little boy. In the morning when I woke up, Luka was already up and about. He had the happiest smile on his face. He gave me a big good morning hug and kiss. I so missed those big hugs. We made tea and coffee and chatted at the kitchen table. It was amazing to have this private time with him.

Later that afternoon, Luka and I were sitting back on the bed chatting and the opportunity came up for me to tell him about the book. I just came right out and said, "I wrote a book." He said, "Oh, that's nice sweetie." At that point I don't think he realized I was serious. Then he said casually, "What kind of book did you write?" He knows I love to write, so maybe he thought in my spare time I had written a personal little book, like a journal or something. I said, "I wrote a book about you." He said, "About me, oh that's nice." He still wasn't getting it. He must have still thought it was some sort of personal writing project. Then he said, "So why did you write about me sweetie?" I said, "I really wrote a book, a real book. It's being published." He looked at me and said, "What! Are you serious?" He just kept looking at me in shock. "Why? What kind of book? Why is it about me?" I explained to him that I needed to write a book about everything that had happened. I needed to tell my side of the story.

He said, "Ok what did you write about? When did you write this?" I explained to him how I wrote from my heart. My feelings and thoughts were in turmoil, and my words were raw and harsh at times. I had to do it, I had to set the record straight on a lot of things, and I wanted to write it from my point of view. Luka began to grasp the gravity of my news. He said, "I understand, but this is a lot for me to take in. I never expected this." I told him that I waited to tell him until we were on our PFV because I wanted to be with him in person and have time to privately discuss it. He asked me a few more questions, like what the title was and when it would be published.

Luka and I held hands, and he told me he understood why I felt I needed to do this. He told me he supported me and that he loved me very much. It felt so good to finally tell him, like a huge weight was lifted from me.

That evening I explained to Luka that my anxiety was up because of this confined space. I was under stress worrying about my father and the other kids, the medication taking routine, and not being able to smoke. I asked him if he would mind if I cut the visit short and stayed two days instead of four as planned. I felt really bad, but I was really struggling. He said, "Of course I don't mind. You did really well!" He told me not to feel bad at all, he completely understood. I told Luka that I had thought I would be able to do the whole four days, but it was harder than I thought. I apologized for not being able to follow through. Luka told me there was no need to apologize at all. He was very understanding and promised me that he wasn't disappointed. Luka has always been a very empathetic person, but I couldn't help feeling sad about my decision to leave early. I really, really wanted to stay for the entire visit, but I just couldn't do it. My stress level was too high.

I've come a long way over the past few years, but I'm not 100 percent. I've learned to recognize the symptoms of my body telling me I'm overdoing it. I pay attention. I don't want to crash. I'm no good to anyone if I'm in that state. So, we had a lovely dinner, took some more pics, and the three of us chatted the rest of the evening. I went for my medications, and then the three of us stayed up till 11 p.m. or so talking.

I got my nice big bedtime hug from Luka, and we all turned in for the night. As I laid in bed that night a surreal feeling came over me, almost a panic. Here I was in the confines of a maximum federal prison inside a caged unit with my son. In a million years I never would have imagined I'd be where I was. The feeling literally took my breath away; my heart was pounding! Reality hit me very hard. I thought to myself, I can't even do two days (even in a PFV setting), and my son will have to do another twenty years! I knew after that night he wouldn't be sleeping in the bedroom next to me, so close by, he'd be back resuming prison life sleeping in his cell, and I will be going back to Ontario, over 1,000 miles away from him. No more waking up to Luka's smiling face and big warm hugs, no more making meals together in the kitchen, no more having my son around me again for another long time. Those thoughts were hard to swallow. I haven't been able to cry in years, but that night I was sobbing on the inside. I was looking out the window through the sheer curtain. The large floodlights lit up the barbed wire fences that surrounded us. I kept repeating over and over again in my head, my poor son, my poor son, I don't want him to be here.

The first thought on my mind the following morning when I opened my eyes was, I'm leaving. What a bittersweet thought that was! I really needed to leave this environment for my own mental health, but I dreaded leaving Luka behind. I came out of the bedroom and met my sweet boy in the hallway. He greeted me with a big smile and hug and a chipper "Good morning, how did you sleep?" My heart was aching, in a few hours I'd be leaving. I said, "Good, sweetie pie, how 'bout you?" He said he slept well. We walked to the kitchen to put the kettle on for tea and coffee with one arm around each other. While I was having my tea, I asked Luka a question. I said, "How do you do this? How do you stay so positive?" He replied, "I don't have a choice. have to be here. I choose to stay positive, and I am happy, very happy." I knew he meant it because he has always been a strong, intelligent, resilient person.

We tidied the unit and started gathering up our stuff to pack. Luka wanted to make a pizza to take with us. As I watched him prepare the pizza, I thought to myself, no matter how long my visits are with my son, they are not enough, but I know it has to be this way. I have to accept it, but it's very difficult at times, and this was one of those times. Then it would be goodbye again.

We finished packing; the time flew by. The guards were at the door to escort us to the visiting room to be processed out. Luka gave my boyfriend a big hug and thanked him for coming and said goodbye. He turned to me, wrapped his arms around me, said he loved me very much, and thanked me for coming. I did not want to let him go. I stayed strong and told him I loved him very much and thanked him for the wonderful visit and the pizza. I picked up my duffel bags and said "I love you" one more time and we left.

A few years later I was back at prison for another reason. The marriage of Luka and Anthony Jolin, who was another inmate where Luka was being housed. It's very uncommon for two inmates to marry. Usually when it happens it's an inmate and someone on the outside. But nothing about Luka has ever been common. The marriage between Luka and Anthony Jolin took place on Monday, June 26, 2017.

Weddings have to take place on a Monday. It is institution policy. An officiant had agreed to come to the institution to perform this ceremony in the visit room. I felt very honored that I was not only the mother of one of the grooms, but my boyfriend and I were both signing witness to the marriage as well.

I treated this wedding just like I would if it was taking place outside of a prison. I made beautiful wedding announcements including photos of Luka and Anthony. They were able to send them to a few close friends. One was for them, and I kept one for my keepsake box. I thoroughly enjoyed making them. It was a labor of love. That's how I cope. I make the best of a situation. Luka and Anthony were so happy and thankful for everything I was doing for them. They both made me feel really special and loved. It didn't matter to me where the wedding was taking place, for to me it was a milestone in my son's life, a day that mothers hope for. We always hope our children will find love and happiness and mine did.

Around mid-May Luka called me to fill me in on some information. He was called to speak to his parole officer about the notice of publication for the wedding. The institution was very concerned that the media would get a hold of the news once the wedding notice was posted publicly. Luka was asked to sign a request form asking a judge not to publicly post the notice due to special circumstances. We thought the judge would be on the same page for obvious reasons.

On June 2 we finally received a decision. The notice would go public. This was not the decision we had hoped for. My heart sank. I started thinking about all kinds of scenarios that could happen if the media got wind of this. They would start hounding the prison staff for a story. They would find me because my name and my address were on the notice. The articles with half-truths, speculations, and horrible comments would be in the headlines of every paper once again. Then I thought what if the media show up in Port-Cartier on the wedding day? That could pose some problems. I stayed positive and considered that maybe no one would even see the notice. Maybe Luka and Anthony's posting would just get covered up and blend in with the rest. Over the next several days I periodically checked the headlines anyway, nothing came up. Maybe I was right? No such luck. On June 20, 2017, I was doing a routine headline search and there it was! The news was out, Luka Magnotta is getting married.

With only days left to go before the wedding, I was starting to think that we were home free with this. We had been sailing under the radar for weeks. In any event, the news was out and there was nothing we could do about it except hope it would blow over quickly. I refused to let articles containing misconceived information, crude notions, and the hateful comments that followed bother me or detract anything from this wedding. We were prepared to deal with whatever came our way. As the last six days passed, there was a new headline every single day with a new spin on the scoop. Some were downright repulsive and offensive.

Luka's husband Anthony is the love of his life, they are incredibly in love and happy. The media started an atrocious lie that Anthony is a white supremacist, which is ludicrous, extremely defamatory, and false. Also, Luka and Anthony did not meet on a dating website for inmates. They have known one another personally for years.

I anticipated that the media could show up at my door over the next few days, but it didn't happen. We left Ontario on Saturday, June 24. The media had not approached me or come to my home. I still thought they might show up in Port-Cartier. We travelled straight on through to Port-Cartier the following day, Sunday, June 25. I was on high alert for the media and curiosity seekers. It's a very small town, and news would travel fast. We were also driving a rental car with the only Ontario plate I noticed in town. We checked in to the Quartier Hotel, the same hotel we always stay at when we're in Port-Cartier. We were getting lots of looks from the locals, but no one was approaching us.

We settled into the hotel room and Luka called me. He was extremely happy that we had arrived safely and that we were so close to him. We talked about "the big day," We had a little mother-son, heart-to-heart pre-wedding talk. After we finished talking I sat there thinking how nice it would be if things were different. I could spend time with him the night before his wedding, and in the morning, I could help him get ready.

I imagined Luka in a top-notch designer suit, crisp white tailor-made shirt, high-end shoes, and I imagined me straightening his fancy tie and pinning a beautiful fresh boutonniere to his lapel. That sentimental daydream put me even more into the wedding spirit, so I decided to go to the store and buy supplies to make gorgeous flowers to decorate the car with. I was still determined to celebrate this wedding just like I would if the circumstances were different.

I got up bright and early the following morning. I had butterflies from excitement in my stomach. I did my hair and makeup and put on my fancy dress and shoes. My boyfriend got on his suit, tie, and dress shoes when I was done.

As we were preparing to leave the hotel we noticed passersby, other hotel guests, and hotel staff watching us. I think it was pretty obvious who we were and where we were going, but no one said a word to us. I held my head high as I got into the car. I didn't care what anyone was saying or thinking. This was a day of celebration for us. We headed down the road to the prison. I could hear the paper flowers I made rustling in the back window as the warm breeze blew through the car. I was smiling from ear to ear.

As we approached the entrance to the prison, we noticed the road was clear, no media. This was good; we would have no hassle getting through.

Upon our arrival we entered the visitation room and waited. Before too long one of the guards came into the visit room and brought a podium for the officiant to use during the ceremony. The butterflies were fluttering in my stomach, and a few minutes later the officiant was escorted into the visit room. She was wearing a black judicial robe.

Anna, Luka and Anthony at the Wedding

We shook hands and introduced ourselves. She was very polite and friendly. I thanked her for coming to perform the ceremony. She organized her paperwork as we waited for Luka and Anthony. I fixed their wedding rings, the two flowers, and the wedding card up nicely on the table. I heard a buzz and a click. I looked up and there was Luka coming in. He was beaming with happiness, he looked absolutely radiant. He was dressed in a really nice white shirt and light blue pants. I reached out my arms as I came around the table, and we embraced in a big hug. After we hugged I held his hands and said, "In a few minutes you're going to be married. I'm so happy for you, and I love you very much." Luka said, "I know, I love you very much too. You look beautiful and thank you so much for coming!" I told him I wouldn't miss it for the world. Luka and my boyfriend hugged, and the officiant introduced herself and shook hands with Luka. She had a big warm smile on her face. Then, we heard another buzz and a click, Anthony came through the door He was beaming as well, and he looked fabulous too. He was wearing a really nice green shirt and black pants. What a handsome couple. I was finally meeting my new son-in-law in person. We gave each other a big long hug, and I told him how wonderful it was to meet him. The ceremony was ready to begin.

Two guards remained in the visit room with Anthony and Luka, and several guards were in the office area behind the glass. We took our places. Luka and Anthony stood in front of the officiant. The guards were within arm's reach of them. I stood just off to the side of the podium holding the rings, and my boyfriend stood to my left, so he could take pictures with the disposable camera. The officiant began the civil marriage ceremony. The marriage was traditionally solemnized with the exchange of "I dos," rings, and a kiss. As I watched my heart was filled with so much love and happiness. I was proud to be present at my son's wedding. The ceremony ended with the joining of hands. Luka and

Anthony were officially pronounced husband and husband. After the ceremony I hugged them both. The marriage documents were signed by Luka, Anthony, and the officiant and witnessed by myself and my boyfriend. They were married! The officiant gave them her wedding blessing, and we all thanked her for coming. She said goodbye and was escorted out by the guards.

The four of us were left in the visit room without guards to enjoy our visit in private. We all sat down at one of the tables and talked about the ceremony, our trip up there, and filled each other in on everyday stuff. We were keeping an eye on the clock as we chatted. Time was flying by quickly; the forty-five minutes were almost up. It was time to start saying our goodbyes. This goodbye wasn't as difficult for me as the ones before. This time I wasn't walking away, leaving my son alone. His new husband was by his side. As we left the visit room, Luka and Anthony waved goodbye, they looked so happy together. I smiled the biggest genuine smile, waved, and blew kisses until I was out of sight. I felt at peace leaving the prison that day. As we pulled out of the prison compound and drove away, I blew the horn just like one does after a wedding.

AFTER

*I've learned in the last six years not to retreat
but to always reload—Luka Magnotta*

In spite of our differences over the years, my son Luka and I have always found a way back to each other because we share an unbreakable bond. Luka is a fascinating person, and I have spent many, many years trying to see the world through his eyes, so I could better understand him. No one knows a child quite like the child's mother, so I can honestly say I know him better than anyone. Luka has lived a very tumultuous life. A life filled with pain, sadness, fear, and confusion; he was debilitated at times as he tried desperately to fit into an unaccepting world. My son doesn't need to search for acceptance any more. He has found something far more valuable. He has found inner peace. The many faces he once donned have all been removed. He is his true self. He is finally comfortable and at peace with the reflection he sees in the mirror. Luka has been held accountable, judged, and punished for his offenses by our legal system that we are all expected to uphold and abide by; therefore, none of us have the right to punish him further. Now that this story has been told from another perspective, perhaps many of the lingering misconceptions out there will be put to rest. Certain facts surrounding this case are indisputable, but there are many scandalous rumors, unsubstantiated comments, and assumptions that are blatant lies.

The repulsive stigma "monster" was recklessly thrown on my son by the media. I am publicly expressing how appalled and disgusted I felt when I read that. I am hereby removing that degrading, dehumanizing stigma that has been pinned on my son. The trials and tribulations Luka has endured willed him the strength to find his lost soul and guide it home. My son is not a monster.

Luka Rocco Magnotta (born Eric Clinton Kirk Newman) is a "person" who is valued and loved dearly by many people. He is somebody's grandson. He is somebody's brother. He is somebody's uncle. He is somebody's love. He is somebody's friend. He is somebody's son. Mine, and I value and love him dearly.

As it stands now, difference of opinion has divided our family to a certain extent. I will never agree with the choice some made to disown Luka, nor can I change that, but I will lead by example and stand by my demonstrated belief that to me family is forever, no matter what. Otherwise I would be a hypocrite. If anyone scorns my son Luka, I cut them from my life.

My investigating hasn't stopped, and it probably never will. The police botched this investigation from the start. The crime scene wasn't secured. People and journalists were in and out taking pics and tours. While Luka was being held in Germany, lawyer Luc LeClair flew all the way there to make a personal plea to Luka. He wanted Luka to retain him as his lawyer. Luc LeClair was determined to be involved in this high-profile case one way or another. When the covert extradition was being planned, Dr. Joel Watts and certain members of law enforcement were determined to be on that flight. They all wanted to be part of the first ever extradition of a prisoner by military plane in Canadian history. A lot of arguing was going on behind closed doors over who got to go on the plane.

Once the plane landed at Mirabel Airport and before they exited the plane, certain members of Luka's entourage were arguing and insisting they wanted to be the ones to walk with Luka, so they could be the ones photographed by the media with him. To them this was their opportunity to be in the limelight.

I've also learned that these same investigators failed miserably at interrogating Luka. For nine hours Luka asked for a lawyer and was denied because the police believed they could break him down, and he would crack and start talking or give them a confession. Luka is very clever; he ignored them for nine hours. They tried every interrogation tactic they had but failed. This is why you will never see the footage from the police interrogation tape of Luka Magnotta.

The investigators never even considered looking at or for anyone else who was involved in this case. Why?

I hope someday Luka will come forth and speak openly about the circumstances surrounding this crime, and he will be taken seriously, and the case will be reopened, and a proper investigation will reveal the whole truth. Luka feels he was victimized by the experts he trusted to handle this case with professionalism. He wanted to tell the whole truth, but instead he was bombarded by "so called" experts who thought they knew best. Apparently, they were wrong, Luka's serving a life sentence in prison.

Every time any information is told what it's like in a Canadian prison guards and CSC try to fool the public about what it is like. In fact, the men are out of their cells most of the time except for bedtime and counts. The men take programs; they have arts and crafts shops, tennis courts, volleyball courts, basketball rooms, a large exercise gym with dozens of machines for lifting weights, yoga classes, a canteen for shopping, a catalogue system for ordering merchandise, access to a huge football field sized yard, a garden and a visiting cottage called a PFV unit to invite guests to spend the weekend with them. Every cell has its own N64 game system/games, CD player and television. Every common room has a television and a full kitchen. They have access to computer rooms and a large library. They have lounges with birds and fish that Luka helps care for. Luka also feeds the rabbits, cats, and other wild animals around the property. The men often suntan and have picnics outside in the summer.

Contrary to popular belief, my son Luka wants nothing to do with the media. He considers it a detrimental entity in society. He considers them judgmental and biased, they sensationalize stories to peak the public's interest and then profit from the misfortunes of others. They are relentless and will stop at nothing to get a story, even if it is untrue.

Luka is not and never has been obsessed with serial killers or violence. There is no evidence of this anywhere. Luka has no history of violence as a child, teenager, or as a young adult. While in prison Luka has been a model inmate. All this hoopla about him and serial killers is made up by people who enjoy sensationalizing and spinning opinions into false "facts." Luka is not interested in criminals and wants no part of any criminal lifestyle.

Many people claim to know Luka or have been in relationships with him. They have nonexistent relationships with him, they come out of the woodwork to seek attention and get some notoriety for their lies. There are many people who claim to be supporters of Luka and try all sorts of antics to befriend and gain access to him. They don't fool us, we've heard it all.

I'm tired of looking over my shoulder. I'm determined to live a normal life. I'm not going to second-guess myself because of who I am. Yes, I am Luka Rocco Magnotta's mother, but I am also an individual person, and I'm proud to be me.

My son Luka is doing very well these days. He has been medication-free for quite some time now. I now firmly believe that he was misdiagnosed with schizophrenia. I refuse to believe Luka has "the most serious" mental illness; yet, he can function normally for almost two years without medication. It's absurd. Luka is in excellent physical and mental health. He follows his correctional plan and is a model prisoner who helps advocate for other inmates. He even found love in prison and has married. My son Luka has found peace, happiness, and love inside a prison; finding that anywhere is difficult to achieve. It's not where you are that you will find these things, they come from within you. As beautiful as it is, it is also very sad. What does that say about society, the world outside the iron bars and gated fences? It's really not as wonderful as we think it is out here. Our world (the outside) and their world (the inside) are in dire need of repair and change. Luka is looking forward to being free one day, and I can't wait for that day to come!

ACKNOWLEDGEMENTS

Words can't express my eternal gratitude to all the phenomenal people and organizations that helped me through the most difficult time in my life! Each and every one of you who reached out and tossed me a 'Life Line' — lines of love, hope, understanding, friendship, assistance, kindness, encouragement, advice ... the list goes on and on — came to me in my time of need.

My father, Walter Thomas Yourkin: Daddy, thank you for being my loyal mentor. You are a remarkable "Miracle Man." You are a stellar example of the perfect father, grandfather, and great-grandfather because you lead by example. You taught me the true meaning of family, love, and loyalty. Thank you for unconditionally loving me and my son, Eric "Luka."

My mother, Phyllis Yourkin (Buttercup): Thank you for keeping me under your wing when I was broken, for wiping away my tears, and for loving me.

My children, Conrad Newman, Melissa Newman, Leo Belanger, Leeanna Belanger, and my nephew Louis Yourkin: Thank you for the long talks, the shoulders I cried on, your forgiveness, your hugs, your patience with me, and your love. My son Luka Magnotta (Eric) thank you for your love, forgiveness, and for supporting me for writing this book.

My grandchildren, Desean, Cory, Royceton, Riley, Emily, Andrea, Christopher, and Danielle. You all bring so much love, hope, light, and happiness into my life.

My brothers, Greg Yourkin and Eldon Yourkin: Thank you for the brotherly love and advice, and for trying to protect me from the world.

My (late) sister Andrea Yourkin: Thank you for always loving my son, Eric "Luka."

My Friend FW: Thank you for being there for me in my times of need and for giving me a wonderful extended family to love.

My cousins, Tim Williams and Tracy: Thank you for all the encouraging talks, and the countless times you were there to love me, support me, and help me to keep it together.

My soul sisters, Kim Hayes and Dee Hayes: Thank you for all your love, support, and understanding and thank you for loving 'our' sister Andrea. You will always be part of our family.

My friends, John and Myra Garrett: Thank you for standing by me through thick and thin, for all the times you comforted me, loved me, and supported me. You both are the definition of true friends.

Barrister and solicitor Christopher Spear of Christopher Spear Law Office in Peterborough: Thank you for coming to my family's aid in our time of need, for your kindness, patience, and for your legal expertise.

Dr. Wendy Thomas, Peterborough Family Health Team: Thank you for the excellent medical care I receive from you, for the incredibly helpful conversations we have, and for all your ongoing support.

My psychotherapist Sheila Collett, Peterborough Family Health Team: Thank you for your valuable advice, on-going support, for your understanding, and for the many hours of much needed and appreciated conversation.

My mental health clinician, Leslie Haynes-Hodgins, Peterborough Family Health Team: Thank you for the countless hours of therapeutic conversation, for your advice, and suggestions, and for your support.

Social Service Worker, Amanda Myles our (Fairy Godmother) Peterborough Family Health Team: I have relied on you immensely over the years; you are magical and one of a kind! Thank you for everything

YWCA Peterborough: Thank you for advocating on behalf of my family and providing us with much-needed resources.

Victim Services: Thank you for assisting my family during our difficult time and addressing our safety concerns.

Detective Sgt. David Ecklund, Toronto Police Services: Thank you for offering your assistance during our difficult time and for all that you did to get justice for Andrea.

Kawartha Pine Ridge District School Board principals, vice-principals, teachers, and support staff: Thank you for your collaborative efforts in helping my children feel comfortable, safe, and able to continue learning during a very difficult time in their lives.

A very special thank you to my co-author Brian Whitney, I couldn't have done this without you Buddy.

Thank you, Wild Blue Press, for giving me the opportunity to publish this book.

Each and every one of the people mentioned above went above and beyond their call of duty. I will never forget you.

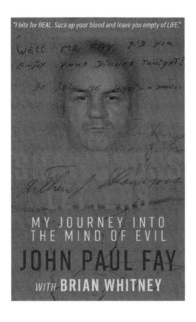
Chapter One
HOW TO SELL YOUR SOUL TO THE DEVIL (AND LIVE JUST LONG ENOUGH TO TELL ABOUT IT)

When God died, the world went berserk.

As a directly connected note and, perhaps, a warning before proceeding, the almost familial relationship I had with Arthur Shawcross, one of history's most terrifying serial killers and admitted (often, boastfully so) cannibals, was a decidedly unholy one.

My relationship to Arthur Shawcross was the closest to a wholesome relationship I've yet had. It has continued to be so. Of course, let it be noted, "wholesome" is a relative designation, as I don't abide the concept of human relationships the way an average individual does.

Not only did I swan dive into the rabbit wormhole, I demolished the only way in or out. Through either willful incompetence, or concentrated free will and accord, to open a vein to attempt an under-the-radar flight from the profanity of a monochrome existence, I made it a preposterous impossibility to reverse course. Whatever, I'm here now, just swinging at the ball as it comes.

The grit.

The grime, the slime, the crime, and the grim, seductive sublime.

The night-washed alleys and sleepily-lit hallways where the dreary, weary, and shady ride out a nod, disguised by their own layer cakes of filth, one get-well-soon spike or dope-sick robbery from overdose or a life sentence.

The backrooms, basements, bunkers, and burnout bachelor pads quietly hiding odd little men who own one too many axes. The secret places unobtrusively blending into the background just out of sight, out of mind.

This is where I live; this is what I live for.

I was playing peek-a-boo with the Devil long before I began my tumbles, fumbles, and stumbles through the brambles of Wonderland and the eerily precarious shores of the abyss led me to Shawcross. Or, perhaps Shawcross, the proudly self-appointed "mutant," was led to me. After all, he reached out to me first.

I'm not entirely certain what this says about my character, but I could never have dreamed how important a figure, at a deeply personal level, Arthur Shawcross was about to become for me. It went well beyond our business arrangements and book agreement. I became dependent on his presence to validate my own minefield of a mind, which was already uniquely primed and wired as unspecified bipolar with antisocial traits. According to a myriad of rather unfortunate psychiatrists I have seen, I am also afflicted with PTSD, OCD, and, occasionally, a psychotic episode to keep people around me on their toes.

There's no denying that inside of me, as my own descent into a Hell-spun lunacy was just getting underway, Shawcross grew roots, integrating into my life as a surreal, symbiotic, perversion of the surrogate father-son dynamic.

Shawcross was the quintessential enabler, a recurring echo goading me into more and more misadventurous indulgences of my tendencies for exorbitantly bizarre behaviors, an ever-present voice interwoven into the hallucinatory soundtrack of my life, founded on the fallen, twisted trees of a ceaselessly treacherous forest.

One or two sharp, brief breaths of counsel here. Don't play with black magic, demons, or, indeed, the Devil Himself, unless you want what you're calling. In other words, do be careful what you wish for. Be dedicated or just be dead. And if you're insane, don't take said insanity lightly. Though, it can, and does, keep life engaging.

Whether ritual magic brings madness or madness leads one to find such things appealing in the first place, I couldn't aptly uncover. In either case, I have my suspicions that Shawcross might have been the ultimate embodiment of my blindly pursuing the darkest of occult sciences, arts, and necromancy, dredging devils from the Pit just to keep me company.

The same reason that I chose, in my drunken hazes, to keep certain friends around for longer than maybe they'd intended. Although the law calls it "false imprisonment," it was real enough for all involved. Certain key details might not be recalled entirely due to chronic alcoholic blackouts, but some graciously administered prescription sleeping medication somehow being mixed into drinks and guests coming out of deep, deep rest the next day or two later, shackled to their bed, may possibly have been an odd phase I went through. No allegations have been made, so this might all be strange delusion. What I can recount clearly was that I was a captive of myself as well, cuffing and shackling my own hands and feet many times over, long before my actual arrests, to get acclimated to moving about with such restrictions. A self-fulfilling prophecy, I suppose. Certainly, I didn't help it not to happen.

When I was ten, my parents pulled their worst off-balancing act up to that point, separated and shuffled their children to any family members who would take us out of pity more than graciousness, establishing us as what my maternal grandmother called "latchkey kids." I felt lost, needing connection to something, someone, anything, anyone. Auntie Lorraine, my father's sister who assumed the role of unofficial surrogate mother, used to take me out for daytrips into witch territory Salem and occasionally treated me to lunch with the witches (I met world-renowned witch Laurie Cabot once at one of those lunches and she very respectfully advised me on a dream potion I'd wanted to try), palm and tarot card readings, life-altering Ouija board sessions, and bought me an elaborate library of books on occult magic and Satanic sciences. My intrigue with the practice of magic took hold of me the way that hard drugs would later. For certain, it was addicting, but it kept a lonely boy busy. My occupation was self-destruction right from the beginning.

Digesting each book, I was especially drawn to the revelation that one could call entities over from wherever they resided. In my reeling desolation, with such an emotionally confused barrier between myself and most everyone else, I thought of it as a friend-on-demand (or more realistically, demon-on-demand). It was hope for something different, something better. My life from the beginning had been a daily carpet bombing of behind-closed-doors abuse and dread, so there really wasn't much to lose.

Experimenting with spells seemed like something over which I could have relative control. It was only the clueless summoning of a randomly chosen demon from a book of black magic incantations, invocations, evocations, provocations, irritations, and optional mutilations. The book was a no-special-occasion gift from Auntie Lorraine, who my parents took full advantage of as far as dumping their children onto, as my "mother" had only had her three children for cosmetic purposes, a sick façade of normalcy, and a pathological need for attention. In the moment, as a child playing with devils beckoning just where Earth and Hell converged, while other children wrapped themselves up in what I considered the most mundane and bloodless of activities, I thought I'd not performed the ritual correctly, or that it simply didn't work.

Much later, I agonized over whether I engaged in an invocation rather than an evocation, or some magical mash-up symbiosis of spells. The summation of said summoning, an invocation is inviting a spirit or demon/jinn into yourself, an evocation is calling these forces outside of yourself at a relatively safe distance. Decades later, emptying bottle after bottle of rum, chasing nearly every mind-altering alchemical substance known to humankind, I wondered if maybe I had not failed at summoning something after all. Particularly, on cocaine I tend to do a lot of wondering aloud. And, may the late-to-the-party Lord help me, I have a racecar-in-the-red proclivity for other radically morbid musings of possibly interdimensional proportions. But it doesn't become overtly dangerous until I remember where I hid the knives. Of course, crazy saves me.

My curiosity came from a deadly serious place. It wasn't only the possibility of having brought an incarnate demon, in the form of Arthur Shawcross, into my life, but some intangible, churning fog rolling with a speed of driven determination, of the most exotic tint of the macabre into myself.

For the uninitiated, the otherwise profane, and those not well rooted to the Underbelly--where even the air is not for the faint of heart: when the wolves are at your door, it's best not to answer. You can't tease demons, who command full-bore commitment. The Devil won't slip a ring around your finger but around your neck. And these forces from well over the rainbow will drag you through the mud like a dumbfounded dog if you're not mindful and always respectful. Candidly speaking then, DO NOT do what I did. Not only did I answer the door, I invited the Beast in with the morbid giddiness of some mad occult scientist. Though, this seemed to be my nature anyway, however unnatural it may be.

Looking back now, that first piece of mail from the Sullivan Correctional Facility was a slow-motion spark heading into a sea of gasoline and dynamite.

6-25-00

Mr. John Fay,

Are you by any chance known by the handle, SAWMAN?

Sometimes I examine who is who on the market. I've quite a list of buyers and sellers. The sellers I stop writing to! That is if the sell my letters to others!

I am leery of who I write to in the mail. Do you know a Melissa from Ripon, CA? I've a few photos of her. I can say MUCH on that one. Let's talk for a while truthful to each other. A.J.S.

Another rule to pay mind to: NEVER take a human skull to a job interview with you. That being noted, it was during the "Golden Age" of eBay. For me at least, but I was bootlegging every imaginable genre of film and auctioning sideshow curios and gaffs including the perennially popular shrunken heads, back when any perfectly sane enterprising capitalist could auction the artifacts of murderers (aka Murderabilia).

For someone like me, who was not all that employable, mainly because of my penchant for trying to strangle bosses, this was a respectable supplemental income. I managed to get my hands on several pieces of Shawcross's artwork (some meticulous 8" x 10" pencil drawings of birds) in a quite amusing trade with a fellow eBayer. She was a female fan of Shawcross and other serial killers throughout the country. I'd traded her a number of homemade video compilations of serial killer interviews, documentaries, and news footage, which I had put together. This kind of subject matter is, as I empirically observed, far more popular than a society of people wearing masks of normalcy might want to know, admit, or admit to knowing.

Financially, it was sensible and sound to auction the drawings of Shawcross' blue jays, cardinals, and seagulls in flight. I figured I would just wait and see whose attention might be piqued, confident that there were other collectors into these unusual acquisitions; people whom let their personas down in the privacy of their hideaways from the world as they tentatively trawled the depths for brushes with evil at a safe distance.

That strange day in June of 2000, when I discovered the unexpected letter from Arthur Shawcross, was, as usual, a grindingly lonely one. Living alongside a shattered and scattered family, it made no difference. We were never on eye-to-eye terms and it's still impossible to imagine how I share blood with such a deranged example of humanity. Taken completely by surprise, after hesitating for half an hour or thereabouts before opening the mail, I had the distinctly alarming feeling that I might be in some kind of trouble. Like the time I was apprehended shoplifting, finally, at one of the nearby malls when I was fifteen. Wrestling ferociously with five security guards, I was eventually half carried and dragged into the department store's tight quarters of a security room. I'd been sloppy that day.

This began with the first mistake of taking my cousin Raymond instead of my usual partner-in-grime Mike, which makes for really bad luck. Apparently, it poisons the dynamic to break that connection. That had been the first apprehension I had the pleasure to experience. What this store essentially did was to extort me for two-hundred-fifty dollars rather than prosecute. So, my first actual arrest wouldn't happen for another twenty-one years, despite many police detainments, interactions, and escorts with ambulances to one hospital or another. With any situation such as this, though, one has an uneasy sense of having the cloak torn off and suddenly realizing how visible you actually are.

As for Shawcross, I worried that I hit an unfortunate nerve with this convicted serial killing cannibal. I also was moderately apprehensive about his having my home address.

A year or two later, chances are I would've taken a blackout cocktail before reading the ice-breaking letter. As it was, I was sober as a judge is supposed to be in most modern American courtrooms, my mind sparking with apprehension, excitement, and, curiously enough, the faint hope that I'd found a new friend off the beaten path.

My policy being to keep as much to myself as was possible, I said nothing about the letter to anybody. It was none of their business. As my divorced parents, who, through some abortion of logic, were still residing in the same ass-backward household, going about their daily scenarios of monotony (my dad continued to stalk my mother even after their divorce, despite sharing the same house), and my two younger sisters impetuously pursued their strapped-for-intelligence boy toys of the month, I went ahead and opened the note. Peeling the envelope, there was a sudden concussive shock that slammed my senses. It was like some innate understanding that I had just then broken the seal on a portal into a deathly pale landscape which should not have been breached and certainly never explored. It was an expression of destiny as tailored in Hell, rising ominously as a duo of the damned and doomed.

Something I have stringently kept to myself was that my usually deadened instinct for brotherhood was buoyed to the surface by Shawcross. It was validation from the pinnacle of we, the soldiers of the macabre; a stamp of approval by one of the world's most unrepentant cannibal compatriots. Could I really have shared that with anyone of sepia-tone sensibilities with the vapid values of a plate of bacon and eggs? Dr. D, my psychiatrist, was already itching to bury me even before things really got out of control. She was a quirky doctor of psychiatry indeed, a straitjacket framed above her desk.

Not that I hadn't recognized it as an especially delicate situation. After all, I was dealing with an openly evil man whose skeletons were so out of the closet that they were re-inventing the cemetery business, handed down a two-hundred-fifty-year bid for a pastime I'd only been experiencing as phantasms, internally toying with for eight or so years at the time, as astounding and frightening in its implications as that is. What mostly concerned me was the prospect of Shawcross being unreasonably challenging. All the other male figures and ass-sideways "role models" in my shit-com of a life certainly were. Exceedingly brutal and mean-spirited men, every one of them. Of course, Shawcross wouldn't be entirely different with his own brand of brutality and intolerance, even toward me on occasion (especially near the end). But we had something in common that I characterize as the "affliction."

How in the arcane name of the devil-headed god Jahbulon of Babylon would I, or could I, respond? Play our words backwards and you'll understand that grim minds think alike, no matter what we try to say in the mundane world to diminish who we really are. I realized later that

I only worried because of that often-crippling lack of self-confidence that stays on me like a perpetually wet blanket, sewn to my soul and not quite locking on to who and what I actually am. I believe that I was groomed for this sinister season, which has really been the only thing in my life I've carried a passion for that was never exhausting to me. The only thing that doesn't feel like work to love. After all, lovers quite literally come and go, whether through boredom or death, but the pursuit of subterfuge sin just doesn't seem to grow old. And it certainly won't die.

I became increasingly indignant as I processed the letter's contents, and lamented that even a habitually murdering maniac wasn't quite catching onto the gist of where I was coming from. A horrible and horrific disconnect, I felt. I did realize how careful I had to be and not write back with a psychotic's abandon. My rants have ruined me for long-term friendships before. So then, I took the path of indignation but ever so delicately. The intentions were to clear up what I believed was a misalignment of communication. If I wanted anyone to understand me, it was Arthur Shawcross. The two of us were companion madmen of the Outskirts; a netherworld director's cut of society, which I had no inclinations of departing anytime soon. As Shawcross had crossed precipices I had yet to, there was something morbidly spellbinding about him. Dare I admit, it felt like an almost inside-out romance. We weren't necessarily on the same page and wouldn't always agree on everything, or ever have perfectly matching personalities, but we were at least on the same bookshelf. An odd camaraderie, I'm the first to confess. These psychedelic shades of gray were never an easy topic to cover with the uninitiated. Not that I wish it on anyone; it skins the spirit bare.

At the beginning of it all, I pitched Shawcross a business arrangement. If he were amenable, wonderful! If not, I'd either get a response spattered with a serial killing cannibal's strain of hate or just never hear from the Genesee River

Killer again. Either way, I was a battered lifetime veteran of bad starts and unhappy endings, so what would be the loss? Still, there was hope, muddied and bloodied as it was.

7/6/00

MR. FAY,

What was the drawing of mine that you sold? What did you sell the item for? I can use a money order -- only if it does not put you out! May I ask who bought said item? Can you send addresses of people who are collectors?

Where might you be moving to? Now that you have parted with one item of mine, here are two more to help you on your way, Mr. Sawman. Some handle you have there! It was the handle, Sawman, that got my attention. I have used a MACHETE on a few...Head come right off! Vietnam will do that to you!

Mr. Fay, I hear about letters being sold all the time. The people who do that I generally leave alone. I dislike writing to someone and have them sell a letter because I have said things that are not cool for the eyes of others!

Wish I was in Boston again. Last time I was there. I was a teenager.

Melissa of California, I'd like to rattle her bones a few times for real... she would not be the same afterward. HAHA

Mr. Fay, you now have her photos. Do as you wish with them.

Stay cool.

Later,

Arthur S.

Chapter Two
DEATH BUBBLES OVER

My emotional baseline, to which I was in agreement with the program coordinator of the court-stipulated intensive outpatient program for addiction and other outlandish mental disorders, was "depressed, miserable, and unusually dark." Schizotypal was among the designated diagnoses that the coordinator gave me, gleaned from the revered DSM-5. Still it was only one facet. Whatever this thing is, it rides hard under the façade. Suffice to state, it doesn't take much to push me past my limits, maybe only an unfortunately timed nudge. However, some of the criteria does have to be taken with a grain of salt. The mental health field tends to overlook anything of a spiritual nature when it comes to diagnosing someone of my ilk, except to classify anyone adhering to such uncanny ideas as being a delusional, magical-thinking psychotic voted "Most Likely to Butcher Every Living Thing."

I did manage to roll past the initial mental tumult and torment of feeling that I'd somehow been slighted by Shawcross, coming up with an approach that might be my entree into ingratiating myself and getting on my fellow cannibal's "good side," whatever that translated to. For fuck's sake, everyone else in my life had a gross deficit in their interpretations of my personality and a line does have to be drawn somewhere. If only I could make Shawcross aware of my own monster, it might be the start of... something. I wasn't just an opportunist, civilian auctioneer exploiting everything and everyone I could for some bottom-of-the-barrel monetary scrapings. Come on, I'm practically one of you! Still, I knew that it would be in my best interests to go about this with a fragile sensibility, as I also didn't care to spook or turn him off. First, I needed to smooth things over. Then I'd go from there, to wherever that express elevator down led. As with anything else, it was a process of increments. And besides, I couldn't pencil in a war with a serial killer into my already erratic schedule of trying to figure out how to sleep on jobs where the neurotic, nitpicking bosses had the abhorrent expectations for me to go a full eight hours without a nap.

Agitated at first, I was on the verge of writing, "Dear Mr. Shawcross, How is my favorite lunatic today?" Instead, I opted to soldier on and painstakingly crafted my reply with obsessive neurosis to make literally every syllable as near to perfect as possible. I was sincere in the expression of my disappointment in Shawcross, his believing that I might cheat him. That just wasn't me. I hustled corporations, not people. Considering it reasonably pragmatic and diplomatic enough, I appealed to the universal love of money. I began pitching my unconventional acquaintance and possible acquisition what might be a financially sound proposal, which was that Shawcross could finagle some more drawings and we could then do a 50/50 split on the auctions' proceeds. It was the shot of a starter pistol to what happens when a pair of cartoonish, cataclysmic characters of undetermined origins crosses paths and never quite leaves each other's side again.

By his second letter, Shawcross seemed to have relaxed, evidently realizing that I wasn't a threat to him, and I noticed that he was gradually less formal. The first letter, signed "A.J.S.," the second "Arthur S.," and by the third, we'd made it to "Art." And he wasn't treating me as a trespassing pirate anymore, which was a real relief. Whatever I'd written had evidently worked. I was so miserably tired of alienating people, for one reason on top of another, that I made the conscious decision to nurture this relationship. My mother you could throw off the Empire State Building, but this was meaningful to me. Besides, it helped that Shawcross never openly regretted my birth as my mother had. Then again, I do welcome doom.

Further endearing him to me, he was my number one fan (even if in a Stephen King's "Misery" context) of the handle I'd used early in my eBay dealings: **Sawman.**

http://wbp.bz/shawcrossa

1.
July 25, 2003

The monster stirred inside him. Most times, he could tame it. Keep it hidden. Silence its screams. But tonight, the beast demanded release.

She lifted her head up. "You're taking too long. I'm done."

He pressed her head back down. "You're done when I say you're done ..."

She wriggled beneath the firmness of his grip. "No!" she protested, forcing herself up from his lap. She stared him straight in the eyes—defiant and unafraid. "That's all I'm doing for you, Devin."

His calloused fingertips nervously tapped the upholstered backbench and his spine tingled with an odd mixture of excitement and fear. The beast was rising. There was no going back. Not now. Not ever. "Rape her," the monster instructed. "Rape the whore!"

*

It had been a long night of hustling for Nilsa Arizmendi and Angel "Ace" Sanchez. Maybe it was the hot weather, but the regular johns were being especially cheap and irritable, and Nilsa was forced to negotiate smaller fees. Ordinarily, she charged $30 for a half hour, but tonight's tricks were turning a maximum of only $20 and some demanded blowjobs for a measly 10 bucks. Like shrewd customers at a turn-of-the-century street market, the johns knew that the vendor in question was desperate for cash.

Ace loitered around the corners of New Britain Avenue, where his girlfriend worked. He stared glumly at the filthy surroundings, trying not to think about Nilsa's activities. He did not like their lifestyle. In fact, he despised it. But how else could he and Nilsa score drugs? The couple's shared habit was not cheap. In July 2003, they were each smoking about 20 to 30 pieces of crack per day and shooting up a bundle-and-a-half of heroin, which translated to about 10 to 15 bags on the streets. Sometimes, Nilsa used up to three bundles of heroin a day, depending on the amount of crack she smoked. It was a nasty cycle. The crack got Nilsa and Ace ramped up and wired and the heroin brought them down. They needed both to survive.

Without the drugs, sickness set in. Being drug sick was terrible—worse than having the flu. In the darkness of their motel room, the childhood sweethearts huddled together in sweat-soaked sheets, shivering with nausea and chills. Every joint and bone ached as invisible bugs furiously crawled beneath the surface of their skin. In between fits of vomiting, their bowels loosened and the bed became soiled. Nilsa kept the curtains drawn and placed the Do Not Disturb sign on the outside door handle for days at a time. The room was a mess. Their lives were a mess. Besides the incessant and all-consuming craving for heroin, she felt shame.

"This shit has to stop," Ace thought as he watched Nilsa emerge from the back seat of an old man's car. She walked toward him, tucked her tie-dyed T-shirt into her dungaree shorts and offered a faint smile. Normally 140 pounds, the 5'2", dark-haired woman was now only skin and bones. "I'm tired," she said. "Let's go home."

On the walk back, Nilsa briefly disappeared and scored a blast of crack at Goodwin Park in Hartford. She returned to Ace and attempted to take his hand. He pulled away. "I'm done with this shit. You gotta go to rehab, Nilsa. We both gotta go."

She acted like she did not hear him. It was usually the best way to avoid a fight.

But tonight, Ace would not let up. "I'm done with the fucking drugs," he mumbled, running his hand through his greasy dark hair. Normally, he kept it long, but a few days before, he had cut it short. "Done with the hustling. Fuck. Fuck this shit."

Their shadowy figures forged into the night, softly illuminated by the neon lights of outdated motels. Rolling hills of forest stood far in the distance, strangely comforting and yet somehow sinister. When Nilsa's high wore down, they started to quarrel. This time, Ace would not take no for an answer. They both had to go to rehab in the morning.

Nilsa was reluctant. She had been in and out of rehab for years and it never did her any good. Still, she loved her four children and desperately wanted to be done with the drugs and get clean forever and for good. Overhead, the night sky opened and a warm drizzle began to fall. The blue rock watch on Nilsa's frail wrist ticked into the early morning hours. They walked southbound along the pike, past Cedar Hill Cemetery containing the corpses of Connecticut's affluent class, including legendary actress Katharine Hepburn, and then a smaller cemetery containing the remains of lesser-known citizens.

Ace gently elbowed Nilsa. "You gonna start singing?"

She sometimes sang Christian hymns that she learned in childhood as they walked along the pike. It passed the time and gave them both a sense of comfort in the midst of all the pain. She smiled beneath the foggy moonlight. "You want me to?"

"You know I like your voice," he replied.

Her smooth, clear voice chimed like a bell into the darkness of the night:

O Lord my God, When I in awesome wonder,
Consider all the worlds Thy Hands have made;
I see the stars, I hear the rolling thunder,
Thy power throughout the universe displayed.

By the time they reached the parking lot of the Stop & Shop in Wethersfield, Ace had persuaded Nilsa to agree to the plan. Nilsa was worthy of a long and healthy life. After all, Ace needed her. Her mother needed her. *Her children needed her.* She vowed to never turn another trick again or inject poison into her veins. The party was over and fuck her if it had not been the party from Hell.

Nilsa eyed a lone vehicle parked in the far corner of the store's lot. "That's Devin's van."

"Let's get back to the motel," Ace said.

"I'm just gonna say hi."

Nilsa walked across the lot to the beat-up blue van owned by their mutual acquaintance, Devin Howell. They had met Howell a few months before. At the time, he was pumping gas at the Exxon gas station on the corner of Broad

Street and New Britain Avenue. The rain was heavy and Ace and Nilsa were soaking wet as they approached Howell's van and asked for a ride to their motel room on the Berlin Turnpike in Wethersfield. "We'll give you five bucks," Ace said.

Howell had to go to Lowe's to price out some supplies for an upcoming job. He was driving in that direction anyway, so it was not a problem to assist two near-strangers who appeared down on their luck. "Yeah, sure. The door's unlocked."

Nilsa and Ace squeezed into the bucket seat on the passenger side. Nilsa used her street name, Maria, when she introduced herself to Howell. As they drove to The Almar Motel, Howell told the couple in his mild Southern drawl that he had a lawn-care business. Ace glanced over his shoulder at the back of the van. The space was large, with a long bench sofa littered with lawn service tools and clothing. The stench of body odor pervaded the vehicle's interior.

When they arrived at the motel, Ace and Nilsa invited Howell into their room to hang out. Howell brought some beer and marijuana. Nilsa and Ace offered to share a little crack, but Howell refused. He was a weed and booze guy. Together, the three got high on their poisons of choice. Howell told them that he was living in his van and he often parked it at the Stop & Shop parking lot in Wethersfield. He left the motel less than an hour later. As he drove back to the Stop & Shop lot to bed down for the night, he glanced at the open ashtray and saw that a $20 bill rolled up inside of it was gone. "No fucking good deed goes unpunished," he cynically thought. Ace and Nilsa had ripped him off.

In the months that followed, the occasional contact with Howell proved beneficial to Nilsa and Ace. The couple had lived on the Berlin Turnpike for the last 18 months or so, first at The Elm Motel and then at The Almar. Their daily routine involved walking from the motel on the pike to the familiar section of New Britain Avenue in Hartford where

Nilsa turned tricks, about 1½ miles from The Almar. Ace had not worked a job for seven or eight months and he no longer had a vehicle of his own. Especially in the cold weather, Nilsa and Ace relied on acquaintances to spot them walking along the busy roadway and offer a lift. Occasionally, they had money for a cab, but that meant less money for drugs.

Howell also proved useful in assisting Nilsa and Ace to cop drugs. He did not mind driving them to local dealers living 15 to 20 minutes away. He would not get high with them when they scored. He seemed content to do them a favor by giving them a ride in exchange for a few dollars. All told, Howell served as the couple's makeshift Uber driver on about five occasions over the course of one month.

At approximately 2:45 a.m. on July 25, 2003, Ace watched Nilsa's skeletal form traipse across the empty parking lot. It was hard for him to believe that this was the same woman whose weight had sky-rocketed to 180 pounds when she was last released from federal prison—all beefed up by the cheap, starchy food. Nilsa stopped at the van and appeared to talk to Howell, who sat in the driver's seat. Then she walked around the van and got into the passenger side. Howell turned on the engine and slowly drove away. It was the last time Ace would see Nilsa alive.

*

When Christ shall come, with shout of acclamation,
And take me home, what joy shall fill my heart.
Then I shall bow, in humble adoration,
And then proclaim: "My God, how great Thou art!"

Nilsa "Coco" Arizmendi, Jan. 29, 1970–July 25, 2003
Rest In Peace

2.

It's a strange thing, writing letters to an alleged serial killer. Stranger still is reading the letters that he writes back.

When I first contacted William Devin Howell in July 2015, he was serving a 15-year sentence for the murder of Nilsa Arizmendi. Howell had yet to be charged with the murders of six other victims whose bones were found in the same wooded area behind the strip mall in New Britain. Nonetheless, the tone of his first letter to me indicated that he knew that the remaining charges were about to slam down upon him with the force of a sledgehammer.

Two months earlier, Howell's image had been smeared across local and national news channels when Chief State's Attorney Kevin Kane named him as the main suspect in the New Britain serial killings. Kane's announcement was a long time coming. Howell told me that two years earlier, he refused to speak with police officers about the accusations without a lawyer present. His refusal to speak resulted in Howell being stripped of his industry job in prison as a kind of punishment by the Department of Corrections (D.O.C.).

While not a big deal to a prison outsider, for an inmate who lives for a few extra dollars a week to purchase better quality soap or tinned spicy tuna at the prison commissary, it was a grave loss for Howell. He took pride in having an industry job. It paid a whopping $1 an hour compared to typical prison jobs that pay 75 cents a day. Howell explained to me that he had worked all his life, whether in lawn care or a pizza parlor or a 7-Eleven in Florida. No job was beneath him and it discouraged him to be sitting in isolation doing nothing.

In April 2015, after speaking with one of Howell's former cellmates, Jonathan Mills, who told investigators that Howell confessed many details of the crimes to him, police obtained a search warrant for Howell's cell at Garner Correctional Institution in Newtown, Conn., where he was being held at the time. The search warrant detailed items taken from the inmate's cell: a newspaper article about the death penalty in

Florida; a notebook with handwritten entries that referenced darkvomit.com, a website that sold memorabilia associated with serial killers and other notorious murderers; and a cell phone bill from July 2003 with words written by Howell, "This just shows the day after I killed."

The newspaper article about the death penalty in Florida prompted authorities to look into whether Howell was behind the unsolved murder of April Marie Stone, 21, who went missing on Jan. 14, 1991, after she was seen walking along a state highway in South Apopka, Fla. Her body was found two days later beside a dirt road in nearby Sanford. She had been stabbed to death and wrapped in a blanket. At the time of the killing, Howell was living about 15 miles away in a trailer in Casselberry with his girlfriend, Mandy, and their infant son. A few months after police found Stone, Howell was charged with soliciting prostitution in Altamonte Springs, the next town over from Casselberry. He had approached the undercover officer in a blue Ford pickup truck and offered her $15 for oral sex, according to the arrest report. He entered a plea of guilty and avoided jail time by paying a fine. It was not until 2015, after Howell was charged with murdering six more victims found behind the strip mall in New Britain, that law enforcement looked into the possibility that he may have been behind Stone's murder in Florida, years before. Investigators in Florida looked into the matter, but did not find any evidence linking Howell to Stone's murder.

I never thought that Howell was behind the slaying of April Stone. She was not part of what appeared to be his target group—prostitutes, many with substance abuse issues—and her body, though wrapped in a blanket, was not buried. Additionally, although Howell had been accused of grisly atrocities—including slicing the fingertips of one of his victims and dismantling her jaw, death by stabbing did not conform to his apparent modus operandi.

I took a deep breath before writing my first letter to Howell, fully aware that I was about to step aboard Ozzy's proverbial Crazy Train with no hope of escape in the years ahead. Here is my letter of introduction:

July 19, 2015
RE: Correspondence and Visitation

Dear Mr. Howell:

I am doing some research and writing about the unsolved murders in New Britain. Since you are the main suspect, I would very much like to correspond with you and meet with you to discuss the allegations. Juliana Holcomb, the daughter of your ex-girlfriend Dorothy, describes you as a "kind-hearted giant." In personal photos, you appear to be a friendly individual who would not harm a fly. I would like to hear your side of the story in this matter.

Please write to me and let me know if I can get on your visitation list. I am a practicing attorney. However, I have no desire to become involved in any of the legal aspects of your incarceration. In my capacity as a journalist, I simply want to hear your side of the story.

Sincerely:
Anne K. Howard
Attorney at Law

And so began my relationship with a man that I believed would one day take the title of Connecticut's most prolific serial killer.

http://wbp.bz/hisgardena

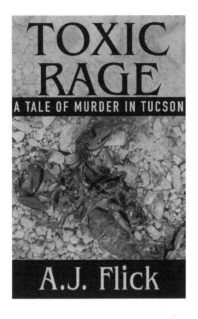
Chapter 1

On the morning of Oct. 6, 2004, in Tucson, Arizona, Lourdes Lopez was getting ready for work and listening to the news on the radio when she heard about a murder that occurred overnight. Her heart skipped a beat. Throughout her law career as a prosecutor and now criminal defense attorney, she wasn't unfamiliar with the situation of hearing about a heinous crime on the news and then having the case land in her lap. But this was different. What few details were being related over the radio concerned Lourdes. They, too, were all too familiar. A man was found dead in a medical complex at First Avenue and River Road the night before. His Lexus was missing. While the report didn't mention the victim's name, Lourdes knew in her now deeply troubled heart that she might have known him.

"Please God," she whispered to herself. "Don't let it be Brian. Just let it be some other poor person."

Lourdes's fears weren't just sympathy for someone who had just been killed, but terror that she knew the killer—a man she almost married. He had spoken often of wanting to have his rival killed … could he possibly have carried out his evil wish? Lourdes remembered countless times over the past two years that the threats had been made and the countless times that Lourdes dismissed them as ranting of a man pushed to his limits. Brad Schwartz, the man Lourdes had broken off her engagement to just months ago, couldn't have had Brian Stidham killed, she reasoned. But the more she told herself that, the more she remembered his lies, lies that led to the doom of their relationship and, perhaps, Brian Stidham's life.

Tucson, for all of its worldliness as a metropolitan center pushing a million residents, still thinks of itself as a small town. There may be drive-by shootings in certain parts of town that don't garner much attention, but this murder was different. It was at a midtown medical complex off a busy street where thousands drive each day. This murder topped all of the newscasts that day and was a front-page story in the afternoon daily, the *Tucson Citizen*. Lourdes couldn't shake the fear that she thought the murder victim was Brian and that Brad had ordered his death somehow. Lourdes tried to go about her normal business that day. She was working as a criminal defense attorney, but she'd spent years at the Pima County Attorney's Office as a criminal prosecutor. That's what she was doing when she met Brad Schwartz, who saved her foster daughter's eyesight, and began an on-and-off affair with him. Lourdes spent the morning of Oct. 6 in depositions downtown, but as she was heading back to her office that afternoon, she got the idea to call Brian's office. Maybe Brian wasn't killed, she thought. Maybe she's just overreacting. It was just an eerie coincidence that Brian had an office in that medical complex and drove a Lexus, right? Lourdes dialed Brian's office, pretending to be a parent who needed to make an appointment to see Dr. Stidham and hoping against all odds that the person who answered the phone would happily make that appointment. Instead, Lourdes heard a glum voice at the other end of the line.

"There's been a tragedy. Dr. Stidham has been killed."

Lourdes froze. This couldn't be happening. This doesn't happen in Tucson. To her. To people she knows. There have been many twisted turns in Lourdes's life, but this was just too bizarre to be true, right? How could someone she had loved so much that she wanted to convert to Judaism and marry have someone killed? If the victim had been anybody but Brian, Lourdes would never have thought Brad had anything to do with it. Her mind raced. If Brad did do it, and her gut told her he had, would he remember all the times he threatened to kill Brian in front of her?

"I'm gonna fucking get him," Brad had said to her earlier that year. "That fucking guy's gonna die. He's gonna fucking die."

Brad, a talented eye surgeon with a once-thriving practice, had brought Brian to Tucson from Texas to take over the children's eye surgery while Brad focused on the adults and other pursuits, such as plastic surgery. But the deal went bad when Brad was caught writing illegal prescriptions for Vicodin, a growing addiction to soothe his own shoulder injury (Lourdes had filled some of the prescriptions and was asked to leave the prosecutors' office when she was charged along with Brad in federal court). While Brad was in court-ordered rehab, he turned the entire practice over to Brian. Instead of maintaining Brad's lucrative practice, Brian decided to go off on his own. That infuriated Brad, and in the two years since, it had become his obsession to seek revenge. Sometimes, Brad had said he wanted Brian humiliated—perhaps by someone finding child pornography in his office. But other times, the threats were intimately sinister, including talk of having Brian killed at his new office and have it look like a break-in or fatal carjacking. By the time Lourdes and Brad broke up in May, his threats against Brian occurred almost nightly.

The more Lourdes thought about it, the more she convinced herself that Brad had somehow ordered Brian's death. She wondered if he was crazed enough to have Brian killed, would he want people eliminated who had heard him talk about it? Lourdes's name had to be on top of that list. Lourdes called her brother-in-law and asked him to stay at her house that night, just in case Brad came over and threatened her or the kids.

Lourdes, who knew Brad Schwartz better than anybody, knew it was just a matter of time before he made contact with her. The night after Brian Stidham's murder, he called and asked to come over.

"I need to show you something," Brad said. "I need to come over."

Despite her misgivings, Lourdes allowed him into her home, where he called up news reports about the murder on her computer.

"I didn't have anything to do with that, Lourdes," he said.

"I need you to leave my house," Lourdes said, trying to hold her ground.

"OK, OK," Brad said. "But please, Lourdes, come outside with me. Please."

Lourdes followed Brad out, but kept within eyeshot of her brother-in-law, in case she needed his help.

"Lourdes," Brad said. "I had nothing to do with it. Look me in the eyes. Lourdes, I didn't do anything."

"Please," Lourdes begged. "Please, Brad, just go."

Lourdes *knew* that Brad had Brian killed. She didn't know exactly how, but what really scared her was what she should do now. To have Brad hounding her for sympathy, for support, was only confusing her and adding to her agony. Typically for Brad, he called her constantly from that night on.

"I need a friend to talk to," he pleaded with her. "You are my friend. I need you. This is such a hard time for me."

Lourdes knew that she was Brad's only friend. He trusted her. But did she trust him? Their relationship began with a lie—Brad told her he was divorced, but he wasn't. Their affair—one of many Brad had throughout his marriage—led to his divorce. Lourdes knew that Brad wasn't faithful to her, too. So Brad lied to her. Brad dragged her down into the rapidly spinning decline of his personal and professional life, thus forever altering hers. Does this mean he's capable of having someone killed? As much as Lourdes didn't want to believe it, she was certain he did have Brian Stidham killed. But she also still loved Brad Schwartz. She couldn't trust him, and she wouldn't marry him, but could she hurt the man she loved by accusing him of cold-blooded murder? Brian Stidham, the talented eye surgeon and young husband and father of two, was dead and didn't deserve to die by someone else's hand. What would she do? What could she do? Lourdes just didn't want to believe that his threats were true—because had she taken them seriously, would Brian Stidham still be alive? Lourdes spent her days defending criminals accused of horrible crimes. Could she have let a killer get so close to her without knowing what his intentions were? Should she call the police? Brad denied anything having to do with Brian's death. But Lourdes knew he did.

She just wasn't sure what she should do. So, for now, she did nothing.

Chapter 2

There's an inside joke in Tucson that nobody here is a native. Of course, that's not true, but you can talk to hundreds of people before you find someone who was actually born and raised in the Old Pueblo. In the 1940s and 1950s, swarms of Easterners descended upon Arizona for health reasons. The dry desert air was considered much better for those plagued by lung problems. That no longer was true in the last half of the 20th century as those transplanted Easterners often brought with them all the non-native plants that caused allergic reactions in the first place. Still, Arizona keeps attracting its share of visitors who prefer the "dry heat" and—most prominently—its mild winters to the humid summers and snowy winters of other regions. Winter visitors—snowbirds, Arizona residents call them, sometimes not in an endearing way—often set up houses in the desert as well as their hometown. Many visitors fall in love with the desert so much that they end up moving there. Tucson is no exception. Bounded by the Catalina Mountains on the north, the Rincons on the east and south and the Tucson Mountains on the west, it's a growing community bordering on a 1 million population mark, but still considers itself a small town.

Brad Schwartz probably never dreamed that he'd live in a place so different than New York. Staten Island, N.Y., has had a small, but thriving, Jewish community since the turn of the 20th century. Adding to that, many Jewish families moved from other New York boroughs to Staten Island in the mid-1960s as the island's farms gave way to developments, thanks in large part to the opening of the Verrazano-Narrows Bridge in 1964 that linked the island and Brooklyn. Henry and Lois Schwartz were one such couple. Bradley Alan Schwartz was born on Jan. 14, 1965, in Brooklyn, but spent his youth on Staten Island.

The Schwartzes kept Kosher, meaning that they adhered to the dietary restrictions of the Jewish faith. The Schwartz kitchen had different sets of dishes, cooking utensils and pans and silverware for meat and dairy products. This is a tradition that Brad Schwartz maintained through his adult life, at least as far as his family life went. Those who dined with Schwartz and his family found that innocently mixing the dishes would arouse Brad's anger.

Henry Schwartz taught social studies, geography, economics and political science to high school students in the New York City public school system for 35 years until he retired in July 1996. His wife, Lois, worked in the administration at a large brokerage firm for 10 years until she retired. Henry and Lois Schwartz were determined to put their children through college, which Henry admits wasn't easy on a teacher's salary. Henry and Lois Schwartz eventually moved to Florida near their daughter, who became a nurse and had two children, one with autistic tendencies. The retired Schwartzes became very active in the lives of their two Florida grandchildren and their three Arizona grandchildren as much as they could, they say.

Later, Brad Schwartz would say that there was no type of abuse or neglect during his childhood and no one in the family had ever been involved in the criminal justice system. As a boy, Brad showed interest in baseball and basketball and the Boy Scouts. Eventually, he achieved the rank of Eagle Scout.

Brad attended public schools until he was enrolled in a private religious high school in New Jersey. After graduating from high school in 1983, Brad enrolled in the

State University of New York at Binghamton, where he studied history and math and graduated at the top of his class in 1987. He was accepted into the University of Rochester's School of Medicine, where he graduated in 1991.

While at Rochester, Brad met and married Joan Samuels, who graduated from the private university's prestigious Institute of Optics. The couple was married on May 3, 1991, in Cedarhurst, N.Y. The young Schwartzes set off for Norwalk, Conn., where Brad accepted an internship in internal medicine at Norwalk Hospital. After that, Brad became a resident in ophthalmology at the Medical College of Virginia in Richmond, where the couple's first two children were born, Ariel in August 1992 and Rayna in June 1995. In Brad's last year in Richmond, he was chief resident of the ophthalmology department. While in Richmond, Brad began suffering tremendous dental pain that required a total of eight root canal surgeries, two extractions and surgery on his jaw and sinuses. Despite the medical treatments that included prescription painkillers, his pain wouldn't go away.

Once Brad was given a fellowship in pediatric ophthalmology at the Wills Eye Hospital in 1995 in Philadelphia, Joan was free to abandon her optical engineering career for full-time motherhood. A year later in July 1996, Brad accepted a second fellowship in neuro-ophthalmology at Allegheny General Hospital in Pittsburgh, where he remained in the ophthalmology department until the middle of 1998.

Perhaps in part lured by warmer climes and the fact that Tucson is the hub of the optics industry, Brad and Joan Schwartz then moved to Arizona, where he accepted a position from a Phoenix-based ophthalmology group to open a southern Arizona office. Brad planned to take the town by storm—and he did. But in the process, some say, he rattled a few too many cages. The stage was then set for the crest of Brad's professional life and the resounding crash of his personal life.

Chapter 3

Far from the urban clatter of New York City's boroughs sits the sleepy East Texas town of Longview. Like many Southwestern cities, Longview owes its life to the railroad.

Brian Stidham and his friends, who grew up in the 1970s thinking they lived in Dullsville, might have been shocked to know that Longview once was a rowdy railroad town with about half the early town comprised of saloons and gambling dens. The notorious bank-robbing Dalton Gang once visited Longview in its early days—and was subsequently run out of town on horseback by gun-toting residents. The public school system that Brian, born Aug. 13, 1967, attended experienced a growth spurt in the 1950s, but his high school wasn't integrated until the fall of 1970. When Brian was a toddler in 1969, optimistic city leaders hoped Longview's population would crest to 116,000 by 1985. But when Brian and his friends became Longview High School's Class of 1985, the town numbered around 75,000.

"It's 75,000 and holding," says Porter Howell, a musician who grew up in Longview and later met Brian through a mutual Longview friend. "Nothing changes."

Many of the kids who attend Longview's public schools keep their friends for a lifetime. For Brian, his closest circle of friends merged in the eighth grade. Brian grew up in a supportive but ambitious family. He was named after his Uncle David, but never called David. Whatever Brian put his mind to he accomplished. For instance, Brian was not a natural musician. But he wanted to play the drums and by the time he was in middle school, intimidated rival drummers including Duane Propes. Propes was in the eighth grade at

Judson Middle School when he first encountered Brian, who was playing drums for the Forest Park Middle School band.

"He used to whip my butt," Duane told the *Tucson Citizen*.

When the two boys were sent to Longview High School, they called a truce.

"It took us by complete surprise that we got to be buddies," said Duane, who later co-founded the hit country band Little Texas along with Porter Howell.

"We had a common bond," Duane said. "But he was so nice about it. We just hit it off."

Music came naturally to Duane, not Brian.

"They called me the wonder drummer," said Duane. "But he had to fight tooth and nail to compete.

"But he worked his tail off to be perfect, and by our senior year he was all-state, and I was the alternate second chair," Duane recalled. "I had to go sit in the audience and watch him with his mom and dad."

Any jealousy Duane might have felt was overpowered by friendship for the shy doctor-to-be.

"We became best friends and every day, we'd hang out together," Duane said.

With their mutual friend, Joe Little, Brian and Duane enjoyed the small delights of their small East Texas hometown.

"We washed his truck, hung out, spent a lot of time doing homework, running around," Duane recalled. (So far as anyone knows, the only time Brian got into trouble with the law was when he was caught with liquor at age 20 in Georgia. His prosecution was deferred, according to the Texas State Board of Medical Examiners, which licenses physicians.)

Hanging out together included sharing big dreams of their futures.

"When we were probably freshmen, everybody knew that Brian was going to be a doctor, Joe Little was going to be a lawyer, and I was going to be a musician," Duane said. "It was in the cards, and it was exactly what happened."

Coming of age in Longview in the 1980s wasn't always as boring as Brian and his friends imagined it to be.

"Longview High School could be a dangerous place," Duane recalled. "There were fights all the time. We grew up in that time where somebody would say, 'I'm gonna kick your ass,' you say, 'Well, all right, where do you want to do this?'"

Brian wasn't the kind of person who went around looking for fights, his friend said.

"Neither one of us were fighters," Duane said. "I think the last fight Brian was in was in the seventh grade."

By pursuing a career in medicine, Brian was following a family tradition. His namesake uncle was a physician as was his grandfather.

"It was just what he wanted to do," Duane said. "He had a calling.

"But he was a genius at that. He could do it easy," Duane added.

After Brian and Duane graduated from high school in 1985, they headed to Nashville together, where Brian enrolled in Vanderbilt University and Duane signed up at neighboring Belmont University. The two friends saw each other often during those early college years. Their college graduation would change all that, though, as Brian left Nashville to attend Harvard University's medical school. While Brian was fast-tracking through Harvard—graduating in three years—Duane and Porter Howell formed Little Texas with other Lone Star state refugees. Just as Little Texas was beginning to hit the charts, Brian was working in the residency program for internal medicine at Texas Southwestern Medical School in Dallas.

One year after arriving in Dallas, Brian switched from internal medicine to ophthalmology.

"Brian could have been a brilliant cancer research scientist," Duane said, adding that his friend spent a summer at the prestigious Johns Hopkins University.

Internal medicine meant too many emergencies, Brian figured.

"He told me he went into pediatric ophthalmology because he didn't want the phone to be ringing in the middle of the night," Duane said. "And he just loved kids so much."

Soon, Brian was ready to make a lifetime commitment of another sort: Marriage. He had noticed a pretty neighbor— "Brian never hung out with ugly women, I'll give him that!" Duane said—named Daphne Herding.

"His heart, his sincerity was so appealing, so approachable," Daphne Stidham told the *Tucson Citizen*. "He was easy to talk to and made me feel so good inside. I felt safe with him."

Brian and Daphne became early-morning running partners, spending many evenings sipping Japanese sake and sharing conversation.

Two years after they met, Brian and Daphne became engaged.

"He was engaged to another girl at one point," Duane said. "And we (his friends) didn't like her. It was, like, two weeks before the wedding and he bailed. It was a big Georgia society wedding, too. He said, 'I'm making a mistake. I can't do this.' So he got out, and we all said, 'Yay!'

"Daphne was different. Daphne is kind of like him: quiet, very reserved. She's a woman of few words. She chooses her words carefully. She just has a very sweet soul and is just a dear. She's hard to describe. She's … just cool, you know," Duane said.

"And, she's gorgeous!" Duane added, grinning. "But you could tell that they fit. They meshed. They read each other's mind, that type of thing."

Duane was proud to serve as the best man at the couple's May 31, 1997, garden wedding ceremony at the Crescent Hotel in Dallas.

After a Hawaiian honeymoon, the newlyweds moved to Indianapolis, where Brian took a fellowship in pediatric ophthalmology and adult strabismus—eye misalignment—which would become Brian's specialty. After a year in Indiana, the couple returned to Texas, where Brian joined the faculty of the University of Texas in Houston. There, he reunited with his friend, Joe, who had indeed become an attorney, and eventually, his musical pal Duane, who was nursing a broken heart from a divorce.

Fatherhood came for Brian in the year 2000, when Daphne gave birth to their son, Alexandre Brian. Daughter Catherine Elizabeth would join the family in 2003.

Ever ambitious, though, Brian was constantly looking ahead. An ad in a trade journal caught his eye regarding a position in Tucson, Arizona, to help a fellow eye surgeon's pediatric practice. Brian couldn't wait to check it out.

http://wbp.bz/toxicragea

More True Crime You'll Love From WildBlue Press

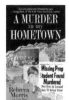

A MURDER IN MY HOMETOWN by Rebecca Morris

Nearly 50 years after the murder of seventeen year old Dick Kitchel, Rebecca Morris returned to her hometown to write about how the murder changed a town, a school, and the lives of his friends.

wbp.bz/hometowna

THE BEAST I LOVED by Robert Davidson

Robert Davidson again demonstrates that he is a master of psychological horror in this riveting and hypnotic story ... I was so enthralled that I finished the book in a single sitting. "—James Byron Huggins, International Bestselling Author of The Reckoning

wbp.bz/tbila

BULLIED TO DEATH by Judith A. Yates

On September 5, 2015, in a public park in LaVergne, Tennessee, fourteen-year-old Sherokee Harriman drove a kitchen knife into her stomach as other teens watched in horror. Despite attempts to save her, the girl died, and the coroner ruled it a "suicide." But was it? Or was it a crime perpetuated by other teens who had bullied her?

wbp.bz/btda

SUMMARY EXECUTION by Michael Withey

"An incredible true story that reads like an international crime thriller peopled with assassins, political activists, shady FBI informants, murdered witnesses, a tenacious attorney, and a murderous foreign dictator."—Steve Jackson, New York Times bestselling author of NO STONE UNTURNED

wbp.bz/sea

Manufactured by Amazon.ca
Bolton, ON